6565

6565

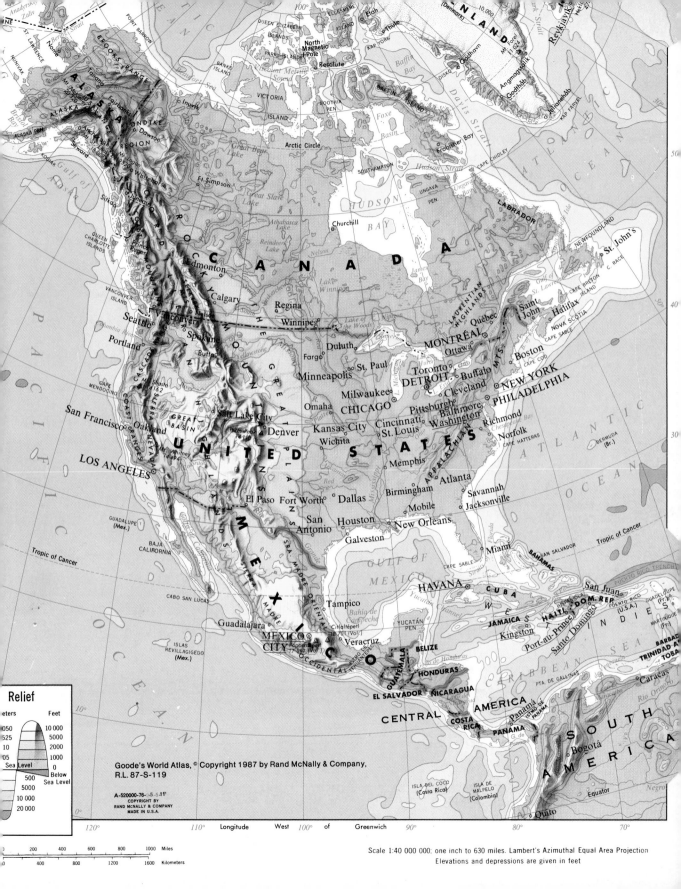

Anadyrskiy Zaliv

Bering Strait

POINT BARROW

BROOKS RANGE

ALASKA

ALEUTIAN

ALASKA PEN.

KODIAK I.

Gulf of Alaska

Seward

Sitka

Juneau

Whitehorse

KLONDIKE REGION

Dawson

ROCKY

Prince Rupert

QUEEN CHARLOTTE ISLANDS

CAPE MENDOCINO

VANCOUVER ISLAND

Vancouver

Seattle

Portland

Spokane

Butte

CASCADE MTS.

COAST RANGES

San Francisco

Oakland

Mt. Shasta 14162

SIERRA NEVADA

Mt. Whitney 14494

LOS ANGELES

GUADALUPE (Mex.)

BAJA CALIFORNIA

CABO SAN LUCAS

ISLAS REVILLAGIGEDO (Mex.)

Tropic of Cancer

QUEEN ELIZABETH ISLANDS

North Magnetic Pole

PARRY ISLANDS

BANKS ISLAND

VICTORIA ISLAND

MELVILLE SOUND

BOOTHIA PEN.

Resolute

Arctic Circle

Inuvik

Ft. Simpson

Great Bear Lake

Great Slave Lake

Athabasca Lake

Reindeer Lake

Edmonton

Calgary

Regina

Winnipeg

Lake Winnipeg

Lake of the Woods

Duluth

Fargo

Minneapolis

St. Paul

Milwaukee

CHICAGO

Omaha

Salt Lake City

Pikes Peak 14110

Denver

GREAT BASIN

UNITED STATES

GREAT PLAINS

Kansas City

Wichita

St. Louis

Memphis

El Paso

Fort Worth

Dallas

San Antonio

Houston

Galveston

Birmingham

Mobile

New Orleans

Atlanta

Savannah

Jacksonville

CANADA

Churchill

HUDSON BAY

SOUTHAMPTON I.

James Bay

LAURENTIAN HIGHLANDS

Québec

MONTRÉAL

Ottawa

Toronto

DETROIT

Cleveland

Buffalo

Pittsburgh

Baltimore

Washington

Richmond

Norfolk

CAPE HATTERAS

NEW YORK

PHILADELPHIA

Boston

CAPE COD

Saint John

Halifax

NOVA SCOTIA

CAPE SABLE

NEWFOUNDLAND

St. John's

C. RACE

CAPE BRETON ISLAND

Gulf of St. Lawrence

LABRADOR

UNGAVA PEN.

Ungava Bay

CAPE CHIDLEY

Frobisher Bay

Hudson Strait

FOXE BASIN

BAFFIN ISLAND

Baffin Bay

DAVIS STRAIT

KAP FARVEL

Godthåb

Angmagssalik

Julianehåb

GREENLAND

Reykjavík

Thule

KAR YORK

North Magnetic Pole

ATLANTIC OCEAN

BERMUDA (Br.)

GULF OF MEXICO

YUCATÁN PEN.

Tampico

Bahía de Campeche

Guadalajara

MEXICO CITY

Popocatépetl 17,887 (Vol.)

Citlaltépetl 18,701 (Vol.)

Veracruz

MEXICO

SRA. MADRE OCCIDENTAL

SRA. MADRE ORIENTAL

SIERRA MADRE

ISTMO DE TEHUANTEPEC

GUATEMALA

BELIZE

HONDURAS

EL SALVADOR

NICARAGUA

COSTA RICA

PANAMA

CENTRAL AMERICA

HAVANA

CUBA

JAMAICA

Kingston

HAITI

HISPANIOLA

DOM. REP.

Santo Domingo

Port-au-Prince

PUERTO RICO (U.S.A.)

San Juan

GUADELOUPE (Fr.)

MARTINIQUE (Fr.)

BARBADOS

TRINIDAD AND TOBAGO

WEST INDIES

CARIBBEAN SEA

SAN SALVADOR

BAHAMAS

Tropic of Cancer

PUERTO RICO TRENCH

CAPE SABLE

Miami

Caracas

Río Orinoco

PTA. DE GALLINAS

Bogotá

SOUTH AMERICA

Quito

Equator

ISTMO DE PANAMA

G. de

ISLA DEL COCO (Costa Rica)

ISLA DE MALPELO (Colombia)

PACIFIC OCEAN

ATLANTIC OCEAN

Relief

Meters	Feet
3050	10 000
1525	5000
305	2000
	1000
Sea Level	0
	Below Sea Level
500	
5000	
10 000	
20 000	

Goode's World Atlas, © Copyright 1987 by Rand McNally & Company.
R.L. 87-S-119

A-520000-76- -5-S-11°
COPYRIGHT BY
RAND McNALLY & COMPANY
MADE IN U.S.A.

0	200	400	600	800	1000	Miles
0	400	800	1200	1600		Kilometers

120° 110° Longitude West 100° of Greenwich 90° 80° 70°

Scale 1:40 000 000; one inch to 630 miles. Lambert's Azimuthal Equal Area Projection
Elevations and depressions are given in feet

Enchantment of the World

CUBA

By Ana María B. Vázquez
& Rosa E. Casas

Consultant for Cuba: José Ignacio Rasco, Latin American Transactions, Inc.

Consultant for Reading: Robert L. Hillerich, Ph.D., Bowling Green State University, Bowling Green, Ohio

CHILDRENS PRESS®

CHICAGO

Cuba is a land of many contrasts, from thatch-roofed houses in rural areas (above) to towering, crowded apartment buildings (opposite page) in major cities.

Library of Congress Cataloging-in-Publication Data

Vázquez, Ana María B.
    Cuba.

    (Enchantment of the world)
    Includes index.
    Summary: Discusses the geography,
history, religion, economy, and people
of Cuba.
    1. Cuba—Juvenile literature. I. Casas, Rosa E.
II. Title. III. Series.
F1758.5.V39   1987   972.91   87-10235
ISBN 0-516-02758-1

Childrens Press®, Chicago

Picture Acknowledgments
AP/Wide World Photos, Inc.: Pages 64, 67, 71 (right), 74
(2 photos), 106 (left), 107 (4 photos)
Archivo Editorial La Muralle: Pages 39 (3 photos), 43
(right), 44 (2 photos), 51 (4 photos), 53 (left), 54 (left),
61 (left)
© **Cameramann International, Ltd.:** Pages 83 (right), 88
(bottom), 91 (right)

Historical Pictures Service, Chicago: Pages 41 (2 photos),
43 (left), 49, 53 (right), 54 (right), 57, 63, 78 (left)
© **Hutchison Library:** Pages 26 (left), 82, 102 (right), 111;
© Christine Pemberton: Pages 6, 8, 9 (2 photos), 14, 27, 81
(right), 87 (right), 96 (top), 99 (left), 102 (left)
Library of Congress: Pages 55, 61 (right)
Chip and Rosa Peterson: © Phillips Bourns: Cover, Pages
11, 12, 15, 16, 19, 22 (2 photos), 76 (bottom left), 80
(3 photos), 104, 106 (right), 110 (middle right)
Photo Researchers: © David R. Frazier: Pages 88 (top), 110
(top right); © Don Goode: Page 100; © J. A. Hancock: Page
34 (left); © Fred McConnaughey: Page 34 (right); © Tom
McHugh: Page 30 (left); © Anne Sager: Page 24
© **H. Armstrong Roberts:** Pages 5, 36 (right), 92
© **Shostal Associates:** Pages 18, 26 (right), 36 (left),
58, 76 (3 photos), 78 (right), 81 (left), 91 (left), 99 (right),
110 (bottom middle)
© **Sovfoto:** Pages 28, 71 (left), 72 (left), 83 (left), 95, 96
(bottom)
Tom Stack & Associates: © Jeff Foott: Page 30 (right)
© **Lauren Stockbower:** Pages 72 (right), 84 (right), 85
(2 photos), 87 (left), 109, 110 (top left, middle left, bottom
right), 122
Valan Photos: © Y.R. Tymstra: Pages 4, 10, 20, 32, 33
(2 photos), 84 (left)
Len Meents: Maps on pages 13, 17, 40
**Courtesy Flag Research Center, Winchester,
Massachusetts 01890:** Flag on back cover
Cover: Vedado district of Havana

TABLE OF CONTENTS

Just outside the city of Havana a green rolling landscape begins.

Chapter 1

AN ENCHANTED ISLAND

"This is the most beautiful land that human eyes have ever seen." These were the words of Christopher Columbus when he first set foot on the island of Cuba in 1492. The beauty of Cuba is indeed extraordinary. Its white sand beaches contrast with the light aquamarine waters of the Gulf of Mexico. Its lush vegetation is dominated by towering royal palms, which are found mainly in Cuba. In the years after Columbus discovered Cuba for Spain, this lovely island became known as the "Pearl of the Antilles." It was to become the richest and most advanced of all the West Indies (sometimes called the Antilles). Because of its strategic location in the middle of the Gulf of Mexico, Cuba is also called the "key to the Gulf." This marvelous geographical position has been both an asset and a liability to Cuba. Because of its location, the island was coveted by the English and the Americans while it was still a Spanish colony. In recent years, Cuba has come under Russian influence. Since 1959, when the present Communist (Marxist-Leninist) regime was established by Fidel Castro, Cuba has been a satellite of the Union of Soviet Socialist Republics.

Many Cubans are of mixed ancestry.

THE PEOPLE

Cuba's inhabitants are, for the most part, descendants of Spanish conquerors (conquistadors), colonists and, more recently, immigrants. Many are also descendants of the African slaves who were brought to the island from early colonization days until the abolition of slavery in 1880. A fairly large part of the population are mulattoes, people of mixed black and white parentage. There are barely any vestiges of Cuba's aboriginal Indian population in today's culture, the majority of these natives having died out within the first two centuries of colonization.

Cubans are hard-working people, capable of effort and self-discipline. But they also enjoy music and dancing and are known for their sense of humor and enjoyment of life. The capital of Cuba, Havana (La Habana), was for a long time considered one of the playgrounds of the Western world. Its fun-loving inhabitants were hosts to thousands of tourists annually. For years tourism

The children of Cuba share a rich, diverse heritage.

was one of the country's main sources of income. Since the advent of Communism in 1959, this has changed radically. The Castro government does not allow freedom of travel, therefore visiting Cuba is no longer the attraction it used to be.

THE LANGUAGE

As the native Indians who first inhabited Cuba had died out, so had their languages. After the arrival of the Spaniards in 1492, Spanish became the island's official language. Although immigrants from many other countries have settled in Cuba over the years, the overwhelming majority of both the early settlers and more recent immigrants have been Spanish. However, because the early conquerors came mostly from southern Spain—Andalusia and Extremadura—the accents and intonations of Cuban Spanish strongly resemble the Spanish of the southern part of Spain. The same is true of most of the other Spanish-speaking countries of the Caribbean.

In 1704 Jesuit missionaries built the Cathedral of Havana.

RELIGION

When Columbus landed in Cuba, he proclaimed that he was taking the island in the name of the Catholic monarchs of Spain, King Ferdinand and Queen Isabella, and in the name of Christendom. From then on, the population of Cuba has been essentially Catholic. Other influences on Cuban forms of worship were the Protestant missionaries who established missions, particularly in rural areas, in the early part of this century, and the present-day atheism brought on by the takeover of the Communist regime. In addition, black slaves from Africa brought with them their own tribal religions. Once in Cuba, many of these religious practices were mixed with elements of Catholic worship, and a type of religion called *ñañiguismo* emerged. Ñañiguismo resembles the voodoo religion of Haiti. *Santería*, a cult built around a series of superstitions and religious beliefs, is derived from ñañiguismo. Today it is popular among some sectors of the Cuban population.

Entrance to the University of Havana

EDUCATION

Prior to 1959, the best Cuban education could be received in private schools. Middle and upper class children were often sent to boarding schools or colleges in the United States, but illiteracy existed among lower class Cubans.

One of the main goals of the revolutionary communist government was to erase the island's rate of illiteracy. All private schools were abolished, and a new, state-controlled education system was set up. Education is free at all levels, but totally controlled in content and in scope. It includes preschool, twelve grades of primary and secondary schooling, and university, technical, and specialized education. Teachers, who follow closely not only their students' academic record but also their private lives and political thinking, have become a part of Cuba's privileged class.

At the higher level, Havana boasts one of the oldest universities in the Western World. Although the universities of Santo Domingo, Mexico, and Lima, Peru were founded earlier in the sixteenth century, the University of Havana, which was created in 1728 by Dominican monks and which later became a state university, is a major education force in the Caribbean world. In addition, there are several minor universities in other Cuban cities.

Havana

*A lighthouse and Castillo del Morro
stand at the entrance to Havana Harbor.*

Chapter 2

THE LAND: ITS PLANTS AND ANIMALS

THE LANDSCAPE

The island of Cuba has been compared to an alligator, an old plow, or a hammerhead shark. If you look at a map, you will see why this is so. Perhaps the alligator image fits best if you imagine this tropical reptile with its head facing east and its tail pointing toward Mexico. But, geographically Cuba is really an archipelago that comprises more than half of the West Indies island group. This island group is one of the largest archipelagoes in the world. It is divided into two groups, the Greater and the Lesser Antilles. The Greater Antilles is made up of Cuba, Jamaica, Hispaniola (which includes Haiti and the Dominican Republic), Puerto Rico and a large number of smaller islands. A more familiar name for these islands is the West Indies. The Lesser Antilles includes the Leeward and Windward islands, Trinidad and Tobago, and many smaller islands.

The Cuban archipelago has a combined area of 42,804 square miles (110,861 square kilometers). It includes Cuba and approximately 3,700 smaller islands, islets, and cays. The largest and most important of these, traditionally known as the Isle of

At low tide, volcanic rock can be seen along the coastline of Iguana Island.

Pines, is now called the Isle of Youth for the great number of young settlers who have moved there. The Isle of Youth is an excellent source of fresh produce.

In ancient geological times the ocean covered all the area. The islands were formed by underground earthquakes during the Eocene Period—about 38 to 55 million years ago—at approximately the same time as the Rocky Mountains were formed. What is now the island of Cuba started as several islands. Four of the largest islands became joined as the result of underground seismic movements and evolved into a much greater land form. However, with the increased water level after the last great Ice Age melting, a large part of this land's coastline became submerged. That is one of the reasons why Cuban beaches have a wide line of shallow waters, and also why large vessels must be guided carefully near Cuba's coasts. The four original islands of Cuba are still recognizable by their different geological features.

Varadero Beach is still one of Cuba's choicest vacation spots.

BEACHES

The irregularity of its coastline gives Cuba a variety of unusual and attractive beach formations. Its jagged coastline is made picturesque by the many sandy beaches interrupted by deep bays, coral reefs, mangrove plantations, swamps, and rugged cliffs.

The beaches consist of quite a variety of limestone formations. There are several places in which the "sand" is made up of pebbles, like Pebble Beach in California. The best known of these is called El Caney and is located in Santiago de Cuba province. The pebbles are reddish-brown, giving this beach a most unusual appearance. On the Island of Youth there is a beach of black sand.

The most famous of all Cuban beaches is Varadero, a ten-mile (16 kilometers) stretch along the north coast, in the province of Matanzas. Its sand is so light that it is almost white, and so fine that it feels like silk touching your feet. Varadero is a stoneless

Building sandcastles on Varadero Beach

bottom beach, which means that there are no rocks anywhere. This makes it possible to walk freely and to swim without fearing what you are going to step on. The sea level is very shallow for a long distance making the sea a most lovely light to dark blue color. This beach is one of the most popular tourist attractions in the island.

CAVES

The limestone rock formations that took shape during the Cretaceous (65 to 144 million years ago) and Miocene (5 to 24 million years ago) periods have become permeated in more recent times, which accounts for the many caves that are found in Cuba. Hundreds of miles of cave formations have been explored by geologists, but only a few, like Bellamar or Cueva de los Indios, are open to the public.

Bellamar is one-and-one-half miles (2.4 kilometers) long with vaulted ceilings. It is notable for its beautifully colored stalagmite and stalactite formations and its many underground streams.

Cueva de los Indios is about three-fourths of a mile (1.2 kilometers) long. Its best feature is that at the end of the trail leading through it, you do not have to turn around and retrace your steps. Instead, you just climb into a rowboat and follow the underground stream to the cave's end.

TOPOGRAPHY

Cuba is 759 miles (1,221 kilometers) long, but only 135 miles (217 kilometers) wide at its widest point. At its narrow point it is only 19 miles (31 kilometers) wide, from the bay of Mariel on the north to the Ensenada de Majana on the south. The island terrain is mostly a series of flatlands interrupted by low altitude mountain chains or sierras. There are three main mountainous areas, one at each end and the third one in the south central portion. The lowlands are mostly savanas or flatlands with very fertile soil and, except for the Camagüey region, are interspersed with scattered hilly formations that give the landscape a characteristically soft contour.

MOUNTAINS

The western mountains, the Cordillera de Guaniguanico consists of two ranges, the Sierra del Rosario and the Sierra de los Órganos. The Sierra de los Órganos was so named because its long ranges lie in parallel formation that looked like the pipes of an organ to the Spanish conquerors as they approached the

Sierra del Escambray range

The Sierra del Rosario range

northwestern coast. Its mountains range from seven hundred feet (213 meters) to 2,270 feet (692 meters) at the Pan de Guajaibón, which lies about twelve miles (19 kilometers) from the northern coast. Parts of this mountain range are made up of *mogotes*, which are found only in Cuba. There is no literal translation for *mogotes*. These limestone hills have a flat top and steep vertical sides. They date from the Jurassic period (144 to 213 million years ago). *Mogotes* line the valley of Viñales, one of the better known parts of Cuba.

The Sierra de Trinidad mountains in the south central part of the island include the Trinidad range and the Sierra del Escambray. The highest peak in this range is Pico San Juan. Better known is the Sierra Maestra in the southeastern part of the island. This range extends the farthest and includes such high altitude peaks as Pico Turquino, which rises 6,476 feet (1,974 meters) and the Gran Piedra which stands at 1,250 feet (381 meters).

Treasure Lake in Matanzas Province is considered one of the best bass lakes in the world.

RIVERS AND LAKES

There are many rivers in Cuba, but most of them flow only a short course and do not carry much water. The one exception is the Cauto in the Oriente region. The Cauto River is 230 miles (370 kilometers) long and is fed by many tributaries. It drains the Sierra Maestra mountain range and irrigates a very large land area. Other well-known rivers are the Sagua de Tánamo, the Cuyaguateje, and the Zaza.

One important waterfall in Cuba is the Falls of the Hanabanilla, which resembles, on a smaller scale, Niagara Falls. The Falls of the Cahuri are both notable and scenic as well, having cut their way through layer after layer of crystalline schistic rock.

Cuban lakes are so small that they are really large lagoons, but there is one, the twenty-six mile Laguna de la Leche (Milky Lagoon) that is technically a sound. The Laguna de la Leche is connected to the sea by natural channels, and the sea movements generate disturbances in the lake's calcium carbonate bottom to produce its milky appearance.

CLIMATE

Cuba lies in the tropic zone, but trade winds and warm currents, that later form the Gulf Stream, help to moderate the climate, making it less extreme than that of other tropical locations. Temperatures range from 72°F (22°C) in January to 82°F (28°C) in August, with an annual mean temperature of 78°F (26°C).

There is a rainy and dry season. Winter is the dry season and runs from mid-November to April. This changes abruptly to the summer rainy season that runs from May through October. From late October to early November, the end of the hurricane season, the weather gradually turns dry again, with rain falling rarely. The land becomes dusty and cracks open, grass turns into a brownish carpet, and very few flowers bloom. Cool gusty winds from the north ("el norte") blow almost continually. Then, suddenly, the rains begin again in April or May. It rains almost every day in summer, usually in a downpour lasting from five to thirty minutes and leaving a clear, blue sky. Its refreshing coolness is most welcome in the hot summer days. Cubans are so used to this daily shower that very few of them bother to wear raincoats or carry umbrellas.

During the winter the "norte" makes it too cool for local people to enjoy beach activities, and the ocean waves become more turbulent. But from spring on, life revolves around going to the beach. Swimming, boating, snorkeling, diving, shell hunting, or just lounging on the warm sand beaches are popular activities enjoyed by young and old alike. The only thing that might disturb going to the beach is a hurricane warning.

Workers clear away debris after strong winds
from a hurricane have damaged sections of Havana.

Hurricanes are commonly, and mistakenly, called cyclones in
Cuba. They strike from mid-June to November and can cause
great economic damage and human suffering. Luckily, only a few
hurricanes hit per season.

A hurricane is an atmospheric whirlpool in which the air
current turns at great speed around a center of lower barometric
pressure. The diameter of a hurricane measures from 90 to 375
miles wide (145 to 604 kilometers); the diameter of the center
whirlpool, commonly called the eye, measures from 3½ to 30
miles (5.6 to 48 kilometers).

Tropical hurricanes are more dangerous and more damaging
than nontropical hurricanes. They are characterized by heavy
rains and strong, violent gusts of wind with speeds of 75 to 125 or
more miles per hour (121 to 201 kilometers per mile).

Meteorologists use the theory of fronts to explain hurricanes.
Hurricanes originate when large masses of air from the tropical

22

zones become hotter and more humid than the adjacent ones. This produces an ascending motion in the air that eventually results in the high, heavy, whirlpool winds of a full-fledged storm.

Tropical hurricanes usually follow a westward course under the influence of trade winds. The majority of the hurricanes that affect Cuba originate between June and November. The most dangerous ones are those that develop during October and November and that follow a north path affecting the western part of the island. Reconnaissance airplanes and radar have provided scientists with significant information about the situation, intensity, and course of these dangerous atmospheric disturbances.

PLANTS

Plant life in Cuba is so varied that some geologists have called the island a "miniature continent." There are over eight thousand species of plants on the island. Much of the original vegetation has been replaced by sugarcane, coffee, and rice plantations, but over four thousand plants are endemic (plants that were there when the island was discovered by Europeans). Some of these plants represent really interesting species in the vegetable kingdom. Among them we find the cork palm (*Microcyas calocoma*) of the western region which has survived for over one hundred million years and is considered a living fossil, and the giant cactus (*Dendroureus nundiflorus*), which is found in two parts of the island and is thought to be the largest cactus in the world.

There are trees that are of particular interest to everyday life because of their many practical applications. The most important is the royal palm (*Raystona regia*), the national tree of Cuba. This beautiful tree, tall and slender with its foliage on top, is loved by

The royal palm is protected throughout Cuba

all Cubans and is of great economic importance for the rural population. The stems of the palm leaves are tightly woven to build a typical rural house, while the roofs are thatched with the dried leaves themselves. This offers all the protection that's needed in a very temperate climate. Houses made from the royal palm have been built this same way since the time of the Cuban aborigines, before Columbus's landing. The fruit of the royal palm is clustered in small inedible bunches that are used to feed hogs, a very important animal in rural Cuba. Its oil is extracted for cooking. At the bottom of the palm leaf is the *palmito* that was eaten by the aborigines and by the soldiers during the long struggle for independence and that is now a delicacy used in salads and certain gourmet dishes. The hollowed-out trunk was used by the aborigines to make canoes and still serves that purpose. It is also used to make stools and fences. The royal palm has become a protected species.

The ceiba or kapok (*Ceiba pentandra*), a survivor of very ancient vegetation, is also of significant economic importance. Its cotton-like flowers are used in fillings for pillows and mattresses, and its bark is used for a variety of medicinal purposes. The ceiba plays an important role in many Cuban myths and legends. Under its shade the first mass of thanksgiving was said by the Spanish discoverers and, later, the African slaves associated it with their sacred tree.

Pines grow in abundance all over the island. Several species are endemic to Cuba, like the *Pinus cubensis* that grows in the eastern section and the female species of *Pinus tropicalis* in the west.

The palma barrigona (bellied palm tree) is an endemic species that grows only in a restricted area of the western part of the island. It is a very tall and thin tree that bulges out about a third of the way from the ground, where it collects water. The bellied palm tree has many commercial advantages, as its timber is good for making such diverse items as canoes, stools, chairs, kitchen cupboards, etc.

The yagruma is also a tall, slender tree with a gray trunk and a clump of foliage on top. The leaves of the yagruma are two-toned: dark green on top and silver at the bottom. Its economic importance has died out in modern times, since it was used mostly for primitive medicinal purposes. But it is still romantically linked to the days of the wars of independence, when the Cuban soldiers were nourished by its bark and their wounds wrapped by its large, soft leaves.

The güira is a short tree with long branches. Its timber is not of the best quality and is only used to build such items as animal yokes and fences. What makes the güira interesting is its fruit. This fruit, though inedible, is widely used in making domestic

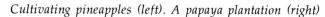
Cultivating pineapples (left). A papaya plantation (right)

utensils like cups and saucers. Its most important use is in the making of maracas, which are probably the most typically Cuban of all musical instruments.

Among the fruit trees in Cuba, the better known are the grapefruit, orange, lemon, and different varieties of the *Annona* family such as the soursop and the sweetsop. An endemic tree that is of interest is the cashew tree. This well-known nut, now a common American snack food, grows in an entirely different fashion from the equally well-known peanut. The cashew nut is the exposed seed of a fleshy, pear-shaped fruit which cannot be eaten fresh but which is used in preserves and marmalades.

The coconut, avocado, mango, guava, and papaya are found wild in every region of Cuba, but they yield a better quality fruit when properly grown. The Cuban avocado has a larger, fleshier fruit than the one found in the U.S. markets.

Pineapples and bananas do not grow on trees. The pineapple plant resembles the popular house plant called screwpine and has long, finely serrated, sharp-edged leaves that look somewhat like a sawblade. It must be carefully cultivated and cared for. The

Young banana trees

pineapple is a native subtropical American plant which has since spread to most of the rest of the world.

Bananas come from a banana plant. These plants are not trees, they are gigantic herbs that spring from an underground rhizome or stem that forms a false trunk composed of closely stalked leaf sheaths. The flower spike emerges from the top and bends downward, later turning into hundreds of fruits. Bananas resemble fingers that are clustered in a handlike fashion. Each cluster, from ten to twenty fingers, is called a hand. After the plants have fruited they die, but they are soon replaced by another one that rises from the underground stem.

There are many different kinds of bananas. The fruit, so well known in the United States, comes in several species ranging from the common one found in stores to very small ones called "plátano dátil" (date-sized banana). There are cooking varieties, plantains, that cannot be eaten raw and are most commonly fried, either after ripening or while still green. In this stage they may be

The fruit of the plantain is a type of banana. Although not as sweet, it supplements many tropical dishes.

processed as plantain chips, or in a thicker version that resembles a cracker.

There is a beautiful tree that grows in all tropical and subtropical parts of the world, the flamboyant. This tree is native to Madagascar and has a particular attraction because its flowers are very bright, ranging from scarlet to orange, and its branches fan out in umbrellalike fashion. Its scientific name is *Delonia regia*, but the French fell in love with its luscious look and called it the "sparkling flame." It is planted in many areas of Cuba and has become one of the characteristic sights of the island, particularly in the Havana region.

There were large numbers of hardwood trees in many forested areas when colonization began. These valuable trees were felled to take the wood to Europe, and today there are many buildings around the world in which Cuban timber was used, such as the famous palace-fortress of El Escorial near Madrid and the Alcazar in Seville. A more common use was for the building and repairing of boats. It took many years for the authorities to realize that the island was in danger of becoming depleted of this valuable asset. A slow process of reforestation began many years ago and has been increased in a marked way by the present government.

Among the better known hardwoods are mahogany, ebony, and granadillo. They are all very beautiful woods that yield excellent timber used for the highest quality furniture.

ANIMAL LIFE

Cuba is part of the Antillian region and belongs to a subregion that includes the Bahamas. The island's isolation has made many animal subspecies typically endemic. Unlike the island's plants, which show large subregional differences, animal life has developed in very similar ways throughout the island. This is mainly due to Cuba's homogenous climate. The main characteristics of the island's animal life are (1) an unusually large variety of species and subspecies; (2) the small size of many species; (3) the uniformity of regional varieties; (4) the small number of vertebrates; and (5) the restricted localization of certain species.

(1) The Cuban archipelago is home to more than seven thousand species of insects, four thousand species of land, river and sea mollusks, more than five hundred species of edible fish, and three hundred or so species of birds.

(2) The small physical size of many animal species is a common feature in Cuba. Generally speaking, there is a size relationship between animals and the places where they live. It would be almost impossible to think of a herd of elephants roaming the narrow Cuban prairies. So it is easy to understand how some of Cuba's animals have evolved into the smallest species of their group. Among these small animals are the ant bird or *pájaro mosca* (*Mellisaga helevae*), the smallest known bird; the butterfly bat (*Nycteceius lepidus*), the smallest known mammal;

The dwarf hutía (left). Manatees (right)

and the sapito (*Sminthillus limbatus*), the smallest known amphibian.

(3) The uniformity of the regional varieties is due to the island's long and narrow shape, which makes it quite homogenous in terms of temperature and moisture.

(4) In comparison to the lower species, vertebrates have low respresentation on the island.

(5) The very restricted localization of certain species is not found anywhere else. For example, there is an archaic reptile (*Crilopes typica*) that is found only in a few square kilometers in the area of Cabo Cruz.

MAMMALS

A striking characteristic of the Cuban fauna is the small number of mammal species. There are some thirty endemic living mammals, but some, like the jutía enana (dwarf hutia) and selenodon (*Atopogale cubana*) are endangered to the point of almost being extinct. There are a few rodents, sloths, insectivores—and twenty-three species of bats. The outstandingly large percentage of bats compared with other mammals is completely opposite to what happens in the large continental land masses—where there are usually far fewer bat species than other mammals. Within the twenty-three species of bats the largest one known is the fisherman bat, because it has a habit of flying low along rivers and lakes and snatching fish by diving. The mariposa (butterfly) bat lives and flies within the innumerable Cuban caves and is the smallest bat species in the world.

Perhaps the most interesting of Cuban mammals are the almiquí, an insectivore, and the manatee, a water-dweller. The almiquí is one of Cuba's largest mammals and one of the largest insectivores in the world.

The manatee, or sea cow, was almost extinct just three decades ago, but a very strict endangered species program has brought it back. For the last twenty-five or thirty years manatees have lived and thrived on riverbanks and in marshes.

The sloths (perezosos) are of interest because they represent a link with ancient continental species. The skeletons of many ancient ones have been found in caves in the central mountains.

BIRDS

More than three hundred species and subspecies of birds can be found in Cuba. Of these some seventy are endemic, but bird migration makes it difficult to determine the origin of birds found in different environments.

Great egrets and blue heron frequent the swamps of Zapata National Park.

Deforestation for agricultural and industrial purposes has greatly damaged the bird habitat. Therefore, there are many species that have disappeared or are greatly endangered. The guacamayo, a beautiful and colorful bird, cannot be found any more, and others, like the endemic parrots and flamingoes, may well be on the way to extinction. This does not mean that all birds are disappearing; there are still a great number of aquatic birds, birds of prey, songbirds, and others. The songbirds of Cuba are admired by songbird lovers worldwide. The better known songbirds are the ruiseñor, which is found in the eastern and western mountains, and the sinsonte, which imitates the song of other birds.

There is one species of parrot that is abundant. It is smaller than the normal parrot and learns to speak very quickly; it has traditionally been one of Cuba's most common pets. The habits and lifestyle of this chatty "cotorra" or "loro" have given rise to many popular sayings.

Birds of prey are found in large numbers. Some, like the tiñosa, (black buzzard) are very useful. This ugly bird doesn't attack

Bird watching (left) is popular in Cuba because many of the birds cannot be seen elsewhere in North America. The Cuban parrot (right) is an endangered species.

living creatures, but instead eats the remains of any dead animal found in the fields. Many other birds of prey are dangerous to small fowl; some, like the cernícalo, have beautiful plumage.

REPTILES

There are some eighty species of reptiles in Cuba, most of which are endemic and found only on the island. Cuban reptiles are not poisonous, and some, like the caguama, or tortoise, and the crocodile are of economic importance.

Tortoises live in the sea and emerge only to lay their eggs in deep holes they dig near the shore. The largest are the caguamas, some of which weigh as much as five hundred pounds. There are two species of crocodiles; one found only at the Zapata and Lanier marshes, and the other, more common one, that lives throughout the Caribbean area. The iguana is a common Cuban land reptile of a variety of sizes and colors. The one that is found in most illustrations, the *Cycluramacleary*, is large and brown, with an upright mane and a rather forbidding appearance. A far more

Common iguanas (left). A dangerous stingray (right)

common iguana is small (from three to four inches long), light-green, fast-moving reptile that is not only totally harmless to man, but is even beneficial, as it lives on small insects like flies and mosquitos that are so abundant in tropical areas.

AMPHIBIANS

Amphibians are equally varied, with some sixty frog and toad species. The most common amphibians are the frogs, which range from quite small to very large. The small ones live all over the island, but are most commonly found in wet areas like marshes, riverbanks, and banana plantations. A bigger species, the rana toro, was first trapped in the fields, and is now farmed and sold commercially. Its thighs make the large edible frog legs found in markets and restaurants.

FISH

Another striking characteristic of the Cuban fauna can be found in the fish population. Though there are more than five hundred species of fish, there are relatively few individual fish within each species. One reason for this seems to be the water temperature. The warmer the water, the lesser the amount of oxygen, and the smaller the concentration of salt. These factors diminish the abundance of life in comparison with the great fishing area of the temperate zone seas.

There is a large variety of edible fish near the coast, but only a few species are fished either for sport or commercially. The better known edible fish include the red snapper, grouper, sea bass, swordfish, and tuna. There are many more edible fishes but these are eaten mostly by the native population. There are also many nonedible fish used in aquariums because of their lovely color.

Sharks are very common in Cuba—there are as many as thirty-five species. Some are not dangerous, but most species will attack humans, which means people should always be careful when swimming in areas where sharks live. Other dangerous fish in Cuba include the stingray, the manta ray, and the moray eel.

MOLLUSKS

There are more than four thousand species of mollusks in Cuba, living on both land and in fresh and sea water. The land species are more interesting because most of them are endemic, but the sea river mollusks are edible, in most cases. The better known ones are oysters, clams, cuttle fish, and octopus, all of which are economically important.

SPONGES

The low level of the sea waters and the general climatic conditions of the area make an almost perfect environment for sponges to live in. There are many places in which sponges can be

Drying sponges at Batabanó (above). Scorpions (right)

found, but one in particular has been traditionally important. This place is Batabanó, a small fishing town on the southern coast of Havana Province.

ARACHNIDS

There are more than five hundred species of arachnids. The most common are the scorpions, both red and black, and the spiders, including the tarantula and the black widow.

INSECTS

Another good example of the great number of lower animals found in Cuba are the insects, more than seven thousand of which have been classified.

The firebeetle is like a living flashlight. It can light a small room enough for people to distinguish things in it. Firebeetles' light beams are greenish, and it is almost unreal to see a field at night where a large number of them has gathered—it's like seeing a city lit up all in green.

Cuban butterflies are so many and so beautiful that there is no way they can be properly described.

Chapter 3

PRE-COLUMBIAN TIMES, CONQUEST, COLONIZATION AND INDEPENDENCE

THE NATIVES OR ABORIGINES

The island of Cuba was populated mainly by two groups of Indians who were cohabiting peacefully when Columbus arrived. They were the Taínos and the Siboneyes. Both groups were originally from South America, but the Taínos arrived later and made up seventy to eighty percent of the population at the time of Columbus. The Siboneyes, weaker and more primitive, eventually became the servants of the Taínos.

These Indians existed basically at the neolithic level and enjoyed a happy, safe life in a land that does not have many dangerous species of animals. They lived mainly from hunting and fishing, though the Taínos had rudimentary agriculture. For hunting the Indians used a weapon called a *macana*, made out of palm trees. For fishing they used varied instruments: arrows, harpoons, nets, and hooks. They also employed a peculiar method of fishing: First they attached a string to a fish called a *guaicań*. The guaicań had suckers that other fish would cling to. It was something like modern fly-fishing with a lure. The Indians threw in the guaicań, waited for the other fish to bite, then reeled them in!

The Taínos built excellent canoes made from one piece of timber. The name they used was the *canoas*, which became the first Indian word that was introduced into the Spanish language. The English word "canoe" is derived from it.

Besides fish, the Taínos' diet consisted of *casabe*, a bread made from a vegetable called yuca; corn, they called *maize*; tropical fruits; and animals like iguanas, turtles, bats, and parrots. The meats and fish were roasted on a spit over an open fire. This was called *barbacoa*, and it is the origin of the word "barbecue."

Unlike other Indian tribes found in pre-Columbian America, the Cuban natives were not very advanced in their arts, crafts, and architecture. They did, however, make primitive pottery out of clay and storage and cooking vessels out of animal shells or carved wood. Their huts, called *bohíos* or *caneyes*, depending on whether they were square or round, had walls made out of the stems of the palm tree leaves and thatched roofs made of palm tree leaves themselves. To this day, Cuban peasants live in similar huts. Inside these huts they used hammocks, called *hamacas*, for sleeping; these were woven out of coarse cotton. The word they used for the tropical storms was *huracán*, and from it comes the word "hurricane."

The Taínos held festivities called *areítos* where they worshiped their ancestors. During these ceremonies they danced and sang, played ball, often got drunk, and smoked tobacco. Most of the time the Taínos wore little clothing. Married women wore a knee-length skirt called *enagua*, single girls wore small aprons, but, for the areítos, the chiefs dressed up in feathers, fish scales, and cotton skirts.

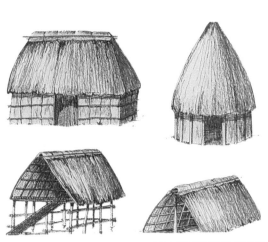

A variety of Indian huts (above). Indian growing maize (right).
Painting of Christopher Columbus (far right)

The Indians were wonderful swimmers—which is not surprising when one considers that Cuba is not only an island, and therefore surrounded by water, but also that it is an archipelago made up of a thousand smaller off-shore coral islands and keys.

The only hardships suffered by the Cuban Indians were the intermittent attacks of another Indian tribe, cruel and warlike, that came from the Lucaya (today's Bahamas). These Carib Indians would land on a beachhead in Cuba, attack the population and take over a part of the area, and, eventually, leave—until the next attack. However, some Caribs remained, especially in the eastern part of the island.

DISCOVERY

Such was the state of affairs in Cuba when Columbus reached the New World in 1492. Columbus believed that he had reached the Orient, where he hoped to find gold, spices, and other riches.

After discovering San Salvador (now one of the Bahamas) and some other small islands, he landed in Cuba on October 27, 1492 (128 years before the *Mayflower* pilgrims arrived in North America). Columbus explored a small part of Cuba, then set sail again and visited another part. But he never discovered that Cuba was an island and, to his dying day in 1506, he believed that it was part of the continent of Asia. (It was not until 1509, when Sabastián de Ocampo, who was ordered to follow the coasts of Cuba, reported that he had gone all the way around, that the Spaniards realized Cuba was indeed an island.) Columbus was disappointed not to find vast amounts of gold as he had expected. He was also surprised to see that the Indians held in their mouths a little brown stick, lit at one end, which they sucked on and then puffed smoke out of their nostrils. They called these sticks *tabacos*. This heralded the discovery of tobacco, which was brought to Europe and became very popular.

CONQUEST AND COLONIZATION

During the next twenty years, many Spaniards came to the New World in search of riches. The man chosen by King Ferdinand to lead the conquest of Cuba was Diego Velázquez, a veteran of many wars and a courageous, though ambitious man. He landed in the eastern part of Cuba in 1511 with a small army. For a while, the Indians resisted, led by a tribal chief named Hatuey. But when Hatuey was captured and burned at the stake, the Indians' morale fell and they gave up the fight.

Hernán Cortés (right) and Diego Velázquez conquered Cuba and killed Chief Hatuey (left), who led the Taíno Indians against the Spaniards.

By 1513, two cities, Baracoa and Bayamo, had been founded by Velázquez. In the two years that followed, he founded five more cities, the most important of which, Havana, was to become the capital. Each of these cities was under the authority of a mayor, who governed in conjunction with a city council. The mayors, in turn, answered to the governor, who was designated by the viceroy of Santo Domingo, an appointee of the king of Spain. The successful establishment of this colony in Cuba encouraged Spain to go on to further conquests, and during the government of Velázquez, Cuba became the starting point for many Spanish expeditions. Having heard from explorers about Mexico and its gold, Hernán Cortés (who had helped Velázquez conquer Cuba), sailed from the island to conquer Mexico in 1518. Years later, in 1539, after Velázquez's death, Hernando de Soto, then governor of Cuba, left the island to conquer Florida. He appointed his wife, Isabel de Bobadilla, governor of Cuba during his absence. Hernando de Soto was never to return to Cuba. After landing in Tampa, Florida, and marching northward, he discovered the Mississippi River, but died of fever near its banks.

It was during this early period of conquest that domestic animals and European plants were introduced to the island of Cuba. One of these plants was sugarcane, which had originally been cultivated in New Guinea, India, and China and had eventually become one of the crops grown in Mediterranean Europe. Sugarcane was to become Cuba's main crop and a source of enormous wealth. The animals brought in at this time were horses, pigs, sheep, bulls, cows, and hens.

THE EXTINCTION OF THE INDIANS

Gold was not as plentiful in Cuba as the Spaniards had hoped, and what little there was in the rivers had to be extracted through the painful and time-consuming method of "washing the gold." For that, the conquerors used the manual labor of the Indians. A system called the *Encomiendas* was established. Each Spaniard was granted a number of Indians to be under his care; these were known as *encomendados*, and the Spanish colonizer was the *encomendero*. His responsibility was to teach his Indians how to work and to indoctrinate them into the Christian faith. These Indians were not officially slaves but, in truth, they were made to work as if they were. Since they were not a physically strong race and were not used to such excessively hard labor, they began to die by the thousands. However, at least one strong voice was heard on behalf of the Indians. Friar Bartolomé de las Casas, a Dominican monk who had come to Cuba with Velázquez, spoke up in defense of the natives and was designated by the crown of Spain the "Protector of the Indians." Despite his efforts, the native population had dwindled from one hundred thousand to four thousand by the end of the sixteenth century. Harsh treatment

Despite the efforts of Father Bartolomé de las Casas (left), almost the entire Indian population died out. Lacking a sufficient labor force, Spaniards brought in blacks from Africa to work the sugar plantations (above).

and such contagious European diseases as the plague and syphilis had taken their toll. The Spaniards, seeing that the native population was frail and quickly disappearing, decided that African blacks should be brought over to work in Cuba. This initiated the long process of slavery which was not to end until the second half of the nineteenth century.

PROGRESS IN THE SIXTEENTH CENTURY

During the first half of the sixteenth century, the colonizers living in Cuba were very poor. Conditions in a country that was sparsely populated and where commerce, industry, and agriculture had hardly begun were harsh. By the middle of the century, however, things had begun to change. One of the favorable factors for change, paradoxically, was the presence of foreign pirates, buccaneers, filibusters, and corsairs who forced the Spanish government to fortify Havana. The pirates were seafaring thieves who sailed under their own flag and attacked

By 1700 Havana (above) was well fortified against attacks by pirate ships (left).

ships or ports to loot them. The buccaneers would land on an island or on the mainland to steal cattle. Filibusters usually acted in cahoots with mercantile companies and, finally, the corsairs were "official" pirates who sailed under the flag of a country; they were vassals of that nation's king and were granted documents permitting them to attack Spain's fleet or its colonies. The nations that were hostile to Spain at this point of history were France, England, and Holland. Spain owned a great many colonies in the New World, and it had established the regime of mercantilism and monopoly, which meant that the colonies could trade only with the mother country. The corsairs were sent, therefore, to conquer or pillage these colonies and their fleet. The most famous of these corsairs was Sir Francis Drake, a vassal of Queen Elizabeth I of England, who sailed the Spanish Main attacking ships and land settlers.

It was this constant harassment that forced the king of Spain to strengthen Cuba, Havana in particular. Huge fortresses were built at the entrance of Havana Harbor. The *flota* system was created, whereby all the ships that traveled between America and Spain did so once a year, all together. They would leave from different parts of the American continent and meet in Havana, after which they would set sail for Spain together. This meant that many of the ships waited for months in Havana for the others to arrive, and that the crews, soldiers, and passengers spent money there and gave it life. Hotels, inns, and taverns were built for this sixteenth century "tourist" trade.

In the meantime, the sugar and tobacco industries had begun to take off. In 1543, the first sugar mill had been established, and, at about the same time, the first tobacco groves were planted. These two industries grew to be a great source of wealth for the island but, for a long time, they were stifled by the existence of the monopoly. This monopoly meant that sugar mill owners and tobacco factory owners could sell their products only to Spain through the intermediary of the *Casa de Contratación*, a government agency that would set the price for the commodities. Timber, especially the beautiful mahogany wood, was also exported from Cuba to Spain. In the meantime, black slaves grew more and more important as a source of wealth for the settlers.

THE OCCUPATION OF HAVANA BY THE ENGLISH

The seventeenth century was a century of growth for Cuba, but one in which the constant attacks by pirates, filibusters, and corsairs made life difficult for the Cuban population. By the end of the century, Spain had become the ally of England and Holland, and the three countries together launched an all-out attack against pirates.

However, by the beginning of the eighteenth century, England was waging war on Spain, and her soldiers attacked Cuba on more than one occasion. One of these attacks involved the occupation of Guantánamo in 1741, which lasted five months. In 1762, England was at war against France and its ally Spain. The British harbored a burning desire to conquer Havana. This city had, in those days, thirty thousand inhabitants—more than the population of New York, Boston, or Philadelphia. A British military and naval force, the likes of which had never before been assembled in the New World, arrived in Havana in June 1762. They were commanded by Lord Albermarle and Admiral Pocock. Havana was not prepared to defend itself, and, after a long and bitter siege, the city fell to the British in August. The war booty included the fortresses, the ships, the artillery pieces, the Royal treasure, and the merchandise stocks that were about to be sent to Spain. The English also became the lords of a large tract of land beyond the city limits of Havana.

During the brief months in which the British ruled Havana, commerce flourished and the enormous possibilities of world trade, as opposed to the Spanish monopoly, were made clear to Cubans. However, after peace was signed between England and Spain and France in 1763, Havana reverted to Spain, and Florida, which had been part of the Spanish colonial empire, was given to England in exchange. Although the Cubans had enjoyed the free trade during British occupation, they had not been entirely happy under it, and they rejoiced when they saw their own Spanish flag hoisted once again.

It was during the reign of Charles III of Spain (ruled 1759-1788), an enlightened monarch, that a series of reforms and favorable laws were introduced in Cuba. While the Americans were fighting for their independence, Cuba was able to trade with them, since Spain was happy to befriend anyone who opposed

England. The Cuban sentiment toward the American rebels was very positive. Money and supplies were sent from Havana to the warring colonies. One group of Cuban ladies even got together and sent all their jewels to the American rebels to help fund their fight for freedom!

It was in 1760 that Spain sent to Cuba the best governor it ever had, Luis de las Casas, a model of justice and honesty. He founded the *Real Sociedad Económica del País* for the general betterment of the country. He created public libraries, newspapers, schools, and a Foundling Home and ordered a census which revealed that there were 272,000 inhabitants living in Cuba. During this time, the great economist and statesman, Arango y Parreño, did much to promote culture in the island; he also worked to gain administrative positions (which usually went to Spaniards) for Cubans. By this time, Havana had become a lively city called the "Boulevard of the New World." According to Baron Humboldt, a German scientist who visited it at the time, Havana was "one of the gayest and most picturesque ports on the shores of equinoctial America."

THE WINDS OF FREEDOM

The first twenty years of the nineteenth century in Latin America were characterized by Spain's loss of most of its colonies. In a short period of time, Mexico, Peru, Argentina, and most of the other New World countries became independent.

The fear of losing Cuba caused the government of Madrid to impose many restrictive measures against Cubans. They, in turn, stimulated by the example of the United States and of the young Hispanic-American republics, started to covet their freedom. Thus began the long, arduous struggle for Cuban independence, a period that was to stretch throughout most of the second half of the nineteenth century.

THE SUBVERSIVE BEGINNINGS

In 1821, a secret conspiratorial society, known as the *Rayos y Soles de Bolívar* was founded. Its members aimed at creating the Republic of Cubanacán, the old native name for the island. One of Cuba's foremost poets, Jose María Heredia, was a member of this society. Unfortunately, the governor discovered this conspiracy, and its six hundred members were arrested and banished to exile. The country was then put under extreme measures of repression. Spain's King Ferdinand VII ordered the governor to treat Cubans as if they were "living under a siege," and they lost most of their civil rights. This did not stop revolutionary conspiracies, and two patriots, Agüero and Sánchez, returned clandestinely and began to spread subversive propaganda. They were discovered, judged, and executed. Theirs was the first Cuban blood shed for independence. Shortly thereafter, a great thinker, José Antonio Saco, who had written extensively against slavery, was sent into exile.

As time went on, the Cuban people kept asking for reforms, and, as these were denied, more and more Cubans joined the ranks of the *separatistas* (those who wanted to be separated from Spain) or of the *anexionistas* (those who felt that the solution was to be annexed to the United States). The latter were mainly rich sugar planters who feared that Spain might abolish slavery. Since slavery was the mainstay of their wealth, these planters decided that they would be better off joining the southern states of the United States, where slavery was still a way of life.

The expeditionary force called Round Island Expedition was led by General Narcisco López (left) to liberate Cuba. The flag of Cuba (right)

The winds of rebellion continued to blow for the first half of the century, but it was not until 1850 that an expeditionary force headed by General Narciso López landed in Cuba with the purpose of starting a revolution. The expedition failed but López, undaunted, tried again in 1851. His men came ashore with a new flag for an independent Cuba (the same one that would later become the national emblem) and a burning desire for freedom. However, they were badly outnumbered. When they did not find enough support among the population, they were beaten. All of López's revolutionaries were tortured or executed, including General López himself, whose last words were: "My death will not change Cuba's fate." An American lawyer in Illinois declared at the time that Cuba suffered from the worst government in the world. His name was Abraham Lincoln.

General Serrano, a liberal man who wanted to establish reforms, became governor. He strove for the participation of Cubans in the government and the elimination of the monopolies on Cuban products, as well as for the abolishment of the high taxation on imports from Spain. A political party, the Reformist Party, was founded during Serrano's tenure. Its aim was to make Spain recognize that Cuba should be like any other Spanish province. However, in 1866, another government took over in Spain, and its ministers openly opposed reforms for Cuba. A new governor, General Lersundi, arrived in Havana stating that there were to be no rights for Cubans. It became completely clear then that only one road was open to Cubans if they wanted rights and liberty, and that was armed rebellion.

THE TEN YEARS' WAR

In the fall of 1868, a group of wealthy and aristocratic landowners started a revolt. On the 10th of October, they gathered at the ranch of Carlos Manuel de Céspedes, who declared the independence of Cuba and, at the time, set his own slaves free. These slaves in turn joined the rebels' ranks. The first of the skirmishes between the Spaniards and the rebels who came to be known as *mambís* (a word of African origin), took place at Yara. Céspedes was proclaimed president of the republic-at-arms, but he was killed in 1874 and did not live to see the end of this ten-year-war (also known as the Great War). It was during this war that Cuba's national anthem was composed and sung for the first time in a church in the town of Bayamo. In different parts of the island, famous Cuban patriots such as Aguilera, Cisneros Betancourt, and Agramonte rose, too, and joined the struggle for freedom. Three

Céspedes   *Máximo Gómez*   *Calixto García*   *Antonio Maceo*

military leaders who were later to fight the final war of independence stood out during the Ten Years' War: Generals Máximo Gómez, Calixto García, and Antonio Maceo. In 1869, a formal constitution was signed and adopted by the rebel government, and the warring republic was recognized by many Latin American countries. It was not, however, recognized by the United States.

In 1871, a crime was committed by the government which helped strengthen the revolutionary spirit in Cuba. Forty-eight medical students from the University of Havana were accused, wrongly, of desecrating the tomb of a well-known newspaper man. After a brief trial, forty were sentenced to prison and eight were sentenced to death. This heinous crime kindled a strong anti-Spanish sentiment among Cubans, and the war went on for seven more years. Finally, however, the death on the battlefield of many of the military leaders from both sides, the impoverishment of the island because of the constant fighting, and the arrival of a new Spanish governor, General Arsenio Martínez Campos, brought about a military stalemate and the end of the war. An intelligent and just man, Martínez Campos offered many of the rights and reforms that Cubans had been asking for, and in 1878, the Peace of Zanjón was signed. However, several rebel military leaders refused to accept the Spanish conditions for peace and left for the United States to continue the conspiracy against Spain.

ANOTHER ATTEMPT AT FREEDOM

Among the leaders who had left the country was General Calixto García. He organized another uprising that began in 1879. It became known as the Small War because it lasted only until 1880. The country was exhausted after the long, harsh Ten Years' War, and, as conditions had eased under the liberal rule of the new governor, the rebels did not find enough support among the population to continue their cause. Shortly thereafter, in 1880, a law abolishing slavery was signed in Spain, though the actual freeing of the slaves did not take place until 1886.

There followed a period of more than ten years of relative stability in Cuba until, in 1891, Romero Robledo was made Minister of Colonies in Spain. Robledo enforced a series of extremely unfavorable measures for the Cubans. The people again became anxious for independence.

THE FINAL WAR

In the meantime, José Martí, a great patriot who was to become known both as the "Father of the Nation" and the "Apostle" was feverishly organizing the War of Independence from the United States. By the spring of 1895, Martí and the other leaders were ready to land in Cuba. They were expected by rebels inside the country, who, led by Juan Gualberto Gómez, had already started

In New York City José Martí (right) and other Cuban
patriots (left) organized for the War of Independence in Cuba.

to fight on February 24th. Against the wishes of the other leaders
(who felt that Martí was the brain of the revolution and not a
military man) Martí insisted on fighting with the rebel forces. The
rebels landed on a beach called Playitas in April, and in May
Martí was shot on the battlefield. The man who had been the
organizer and the inspiration for the independence of Cuba
became even more of a symbol through his death. From then on,
there was no stopping the revolution. For three years, bitter war
was waged on the island, as Spain kept sending more and more
troops to reinforce its army. There were heavy losses on both
sides. One of the rebels' greatest generals, Antonio Maceo, was
killed in 1896. During this time, General Martínez Campos was
relieved of his command and replaced by General Weyler. The
latter, desperately trying to stamp out the rebellion and unable to
do so through military means, created a system called
Reconcentración, wherein the inhabitants of rural areas, including
women, children, and the elderly, were made to move to the cities
to prevent them from helping the *Mambís.* Food became very
scarce in the cities, and many people died. This stirred up the

The New York Journal (left) offered a $50,000 reward for the conviction of criminals responsible for the sinking of the Maine *(above).*

population tremendously, and, at the same time, moved public opinion in the United States, creating a great anti-Spanish sentiment. Eventually, the war would have been won by the Cubans through sheer persistence, but certain events took place that speeded up the end of the struggle and changed the course of history.

THE SPANISH-AMERICAN WAR

Late in the year of 1897, President McKinley of the United States asked Spain to cease its repressive measures in Cuba. Spain, fearing a war with the United States, ordered a stop to the *Reconcentración.* On January 1, 1898, Spain established an autonomous regime in Cuba, but it was too late. The rebel government did not accept it. Nothing short of independence would do. There followed many disturbances in Havana, and the American government sent the battleship *Maine* to protect

President William McKinley

Americans living there. On the 15th of February 1898, an explosion destroyed the ship as it was anchored in Havana Harbor, killing most of its crew. The United States claimed that the explosion had come from a mine and was the work of the Spaniards, while Spain claimed that the explosion had come from within, and that the dynamite had been planted by the Americans wanting an excuse to start a war. To this day, the absolute truth is not known. The American Under-Secretary of the Navy, Theodore Roosevelt, pressed for a declaration of war with Spain. President McKinley tried to stall on such a drastic measure, but on April 25, after an ultimatum had been sent to Spain, war was declared and the hostilities began.

At first, President McKinley did not approach the rebel government presided over by General Masó, but he did allow General Miles, Chief of Staff to the American Army, to establish contact with the Cuban generals García and Gómez. From then on, the Cubans and the Americans led a joint war effort.

The American troops under General Shafter landed in Santiago de Cuba, where the U. S. Navy had already established a blockade. A joint attack of Cuban and American forces at San Juan Hill proved a decisive victory against the Spaniards. Theodore Roosevelt had come himself to lead a cavalry regiment known as the "Rough Riders." The Spanish Navy under Admiral Cervera was destroyed and the latter taken prisoner. While these events were taking place, Spain suffered other defeats in her colonies. The Philippines and Puerto Rico were taken over by the American forces. All this proved to be too much for Spain, and on July 16th the Spanish forces in Cuba surrendered. The official Peace Treaty between Spain and the United States was signed in Paris on December 10th, 1898. The Cubans were unfairly excluded from the negotiations and were made to accept a transitional period of American rule until it was felt they could administer themselves. Cuba's colonial era ended with a feeling of rejoicing, but with no ill-feeling toward the Spaniards themselves. Cubans had objected to the way in which they had been governed, but the cultural and emotional ties to Spain have remained strong to this day.

During the American military government, which lasted almost four years, Cuba was governed first by General John Brooke and later by General Leonard Wood. After the long struggle, the country was submerged in poverty and suffered deplorable sanitary conditions. Much was accomplished by the Americans in the areas of public works, education, and the elimination of yellow fever. It was a Cuban doctor, Carlos Finlay, who in 1881 had discovered that this disease was transmitted by a mosquito. Under General Wood, a campaign was waged against the mosquitos and the disease was stamped out.

In 1901, the Americans prepared to return the island to the Cubans. A number of outstanding men met for three months to write a constitution which, in many ways, followed the pattern of the American one. However, before approving it, the United

Doctor Carlos Juan Finlay

States requested an amendment to it, establishing the precise nature of future Cuban-American relations. The amendment authorized the United States to intervene in Cuba if they felt it necessary to protect the young republic. It forbade the Cuban government to borrow money without the permission of the United States, and it obligated it to lease land to the United States for the establishment of naval bases. The Cubans did not want this amendment, but President McKinley made it very clear that without it, American rule would continue in Cuba. And so, the Platt Amendment (named after the Connecticut Senator who had proposed it) was unwillingly accepted in 1901. It was not to be abolished until Franklin D. Roosevelt's order in 1934.

INDEPENDENCE

In December 1901, national elections took place, and Tomás Estrada Palma was elected Cuba's first president. Estrada Palma had been president of the republic-at-arms during the Ten Years' War and had led an indefatigable struggle for Cuban independence from the United States where he lived in exile. On May 20, 1902, the Americans left Cuba, Estrada Palma took over the reins of government, and the Cuban flag flew for the first time on a peaceful nation.

Completed in 1929, the capitol in Havana is almost an exact replica of the building in the United States.

Chapter 4
LIFE IN THE NEW
REPUBLIC

DEMOCRATIC BEGINNINGS

The Cuban "Constitution of 1901," as it is usually referred to nowadays, established that there should be a change of government every four years. The president, vice-president, and half of the house of representatives and the senate were elected at one time, and the other half of congress and the provincial governors were elected two years later. This system attempted to avoid gaps in experienced personnel in times of change of government.

The first years of the new government, from 1901 to 1905, were employed in trying to get the country going on its own, since it had been under a foreign power up to that time. Improving education and sanitation were the main goals. In both instances a great deal was achieved, but the long struggle for independence had done considerable damage to all social systems.

Social and economic modernization enabled many people to participate in politics. The fact that the economy was basically good during the period helped to create the positive feeling that was prevalent during the time. Cubans thought that the long struggle against Spanish rule and the years of American intervention were well worth it. They had a free and prosperous country. However, this freedom was always shadowed by the fear that the government might exercise its right to ask the United States to intervene in local affairs in accordance with the Platt Amendment. This became the weapon the governing politicians used to keep opposition at a minimum. During the thirty-three years the Platt Amendment was in effect, the ruling politicians exercised this right twice, in 1906 and in 1917. Both times it was in response to revolts led by unhappy politicians and their followers. The exercise of democracy is not easy when it has not been preceded by a good educational program and by a good democratic example.

THE EARLY GOVERNMENTS

The administration of Estrada Palma (1901-1906) set out in a course of honesty and humility. He thought that the presidential salary of $25,000 a year was too much money. His great idealistic aims were to provide education for everyone, to establish meaningful health care programs, and to strengthen the economy. He said frequently that countries should have more teachers than soldiers.

Estrada Palma signed two bills affecting Cuban-American relations. The first one was a commercial reciprocity treaty, and the other granted land for two naval bases to the United States, one at Bahía Honda, returned to Cuba in the early thirties, and Guantánamo Bay. The United States holds the right to stay at Guantánamo until 1999, and apparently it means to do so.

In 1902 the Cuban people elected Tomás Estrada Palma (left) the first president of the Republic of Cuba. President of the United States, Theodore Roosevelt (right)

Estrada Palma increased the treasury funds and governed with personal integrity, trying at the same time to instill this desire for honest government in his government officials. But this was no easy task. There were many ambitious politicians, and the ensuing problems became such that Estrada Palma asked the United States government, then headed by Theodore Roosevelt, to intervene.

The United States government was very much aware of the need to make its intervention short-lived and did what was necessary to uphold this feeling in the Cuban people. They allowed all the national entities to govern. But they tried to please too many interests, and this led to corrupt administrative policies that continued as part of the Cuban government long after the United States had pulled out.

As soon as the political rivalries had subsided, the United States intervening team prepared and carried on national elections. The two-party system was again established, and there were two presidential candidates with similar backgrounds. They had both been key figures in the independence struggle and had held high ranks in the Cuban army. The two parties, the Conservadores and the Liberales, had the same ideals. The only difference was that the Conservadores aimed at attracting the upper middle class voters by promising to uphold close relations with the United States in order to maintain a good economic standard, while the Liberales wanted more detachment from the United States and more popular economic measures.

The elections were won by the Liberales and their candidate. José Miguel Gómez, became the second president. Gómez was a patriarchal figure, and his government which lasted from 1909 to 1913, had that same characteristic. He was a very popular and tolerant president. His main fault was that he allowed much of the government corruption to continue uncontrolled. When his term was up Gómez refused to run for office again.

The next elections were won by the Conservador Party. The Conservadores had promised honesty in government and new sources of employment by establishing sound economic and industrial policies. The elected candidate, Mario García Menocal (who governed from 1913 to 1921) had been defeated in the election four years before. The fact that he had graduated as an engineer from Cornell University, had a solid war of independence record, and came from a wealthy background, gave him an overwhelming majority over the Liberal Party candidate. His presidency was indeed a good one in economic terms. Among other things, Menocal established the national currency and invited foreign capital to invest in Cuban industries—primarily the sugarcane industry.

President Menocal's second term came during the First World War. The price of sugar soared, and because of its thriving sugar industry, Cuba led what was called the "Dance of Millions." Of course the word "millions" refers to dollars, and for a while Cuba

President Mario G. Menocal governed Cuba from 1913 to 1921.

was a very wealthy country indeed. This state of affairs lasted until the end of the war, when the price of crude sugar fell from twenty-three cents per pound to three cents, and the country nearly collapsed.

Menocal's was a good enough government, but the Liberales outnumbered the Conservadores and so had a clear majority in the elections of 1921. Menocal, following ill-advised political allies, did not admit his defeat in these elections, and a short-lived armed conflict started. The United States government, now with Warren G. Harding in the presidency, sent harsh warnings to Cuba via a variety of messengers. These were ill-received by the Cubans, who thought that this time the United States leaders were intervening in Cuba at a moment in which they had no reason to do so. The United States influence changed the way in which the political plans of the country were to take off. Although no American troops landed in Cuba, this meddling so directly in the country's internal affairs was considered another episode of intervention.

Gerardo Machado was elected president in 1924.

And so another Conservador government followed. As the new president, Alfredo Zayas y Alfonso (who governed from 1921 to 1925) was a very relaxed, highly intellectual man; his political life also became calm and orderly. Zayas took steps to prepare the United States Congress to accept the idea of abolishing the Platt Amendment.

In the election of 1924, Gerardo Machado won a resounding victory as the candidate of the Liberal Party. The new president worked hard to implement his programs emphasizing public education and public works. During his term the number of teachers and schools were significantly increased, and the Central Highway was constructed in order to have a road going uninterruptedly from east to west all along the island. He also built the capitol, a magnificent building that housed the Congress, and many other government offices. His public works program included the modernization of Havana and other important cities.

DEMOCRACY TURNS INTO TYRANNY

Good economic and nationalistic measures made Machado one of the best presidents in Cuban history, but he made the same mistake others had done before. He wanted to be reelected. As national policy prohibited his becoming his party's candidate for a second term, he forced Congress to issue a proclamation called the *Prórroga de Poderes* (The Prolongation of Power). This gave the party in power and all its elected officials the power to go on governing the country without an election. Machado took everyone by surprise with such a move because his government had, up until then, brought about such economic and industrial benefits. As a result of this previous popularity, Machado did not encounter true political opposition until his measures became more dictatorial and harsh.

Violence against individual citizens became frequent. The students in the University of Havana became involved. The majority of the student body, with the approval of a significant number of professors, organized a really systematic campaign against Machado and his allies. The students reached all segments of the population. For more than three years violence was a common everyday happening, and student rallies often ended with police and army charging against them. The number of political prisoners, especially young ones, grew daily. Opposition to the government became a way of life, and the quenching of the opposition became the way of governing.

In August of 1933 the student body (*Federación Estudiantil Universitaria*), the workers' unions, and the different groups of professionals called for a general strike. It was successful, and the government fell. Machado and his family fled to Nassau and later moved to New York and finally to Florida, where they stayed until his death.

A period of political unrest followed. There was no provision for presidential succession in case of failure of the president and vice-president, so the chief of staff of the armed forces, General

Alberto Herrera, took over. Herrera was a good military man, but he had no following within the triumphant political groups or with the American ambassador. After only a few days under his authority, all groups agreed to assign as interim president the son of the Father of the Nation, Carlos Manuel de Céspedes. This honest, quiet, intellectual was not the right person to control such an unrestful period, and he was overthrown by the first coup d'etat in Cuban history. The army, under the leadership of Sergeant Fulgencio Batista y Zaldivar, took hold of the government. Batista, a communications officer, did not want to be named president, but he did want to control the country from backstage. Hoping to gain support from the revolutionary forces, he formed a new government headed by two university professors, the editor and owner of a newspaper, an economist, and a banker. This group was called the "pentarchy" and lasted only six days. They chose one of the professors, Ramón Grau San Martín, as the provisional president, but, in the meantime, Batista had made himself an army colonel and had assumed the leadership of the armed forces. The whole officer corps walked out in protest and took refuge in the National Hotel, a lovely building near the seashore. The army dug trenches, the navy sent frigates to the coast of Havana, and the National Hotel was attacked from land and sea. The shelling from the nearest frigate was so intense that the officers waved the white flag. Batista had completely taken over all opposing forces and assumed a role as the "power behind the government" that lasted through all kinds of political changes and upheavals.

There were four provisional presidents put up or brought down at Batista's whim. General elections were held, and the armed forces did not intervene in favor of any of the candidates. But this

Colonel Fulgencio Batista, taking the oath of office as president in 1940

did not mean that Batista wasn't in control. Gómez, the son of the second president was elected by a large majority. He thought that this fact made him capable of restoring the country to normal civil life. He tried too hard, and when the armed forces stepped in, President Gómez was forced to renounce his office. Batista finally became president himself by popular vote in 1940.

DEMOCRATIC INTERLUDE

There were two important points in Batista's favor. He bargained constantly for the abolition of the Platt Amendment that was finally abrogated in 1934, and he convened and carried through a constitutional convention that gave rise to one of the most advanced democratic constitutions in the world—"The Constitution of 1940." Many of its civil and labor points are still unmatched in many industrialized and democratic countries.

Batista was the first president elected under the new constitution. His presidency brought some political stability to the country, and his economic measures were also beneficial. Most of his term took place during the Second World War. As in the First World War, this meant high prices for sugar. Overall, his presidency had a positive effect on Cuba. He ended his term with an unprecedented action from a dictator. He held a totally democratic national election at which he was defeated by the opposition, and he stepped down and went into self-imposed exile at Daytona Beach, Florida.

The new government, the Auténticos, were overwhelmingly popular and had hopes and dreams of a democratic and prosperous nation. But it did not turn out that way. The new leaders were professors, writers, and philosophers, and they did not know how to carry on the powers of the state. Even though everything was done democratically, government institutions began to crumble. Unscrupulous people took advantage of the moment and, soon, even the most beloved and honest of the Auténticos were accomplices to graft and corruption. During this period the Congress passed the "complementary laws" to the new Constitution. These laws imposed checks and balances on the government and were the needed tool to change the nation into a real democracy.

RETURN·TO DICTATORSHIP

Near the end of the Auténticos' second term (1944-1952), Batista returned to Cuba. Then, on March 10, 1952, he master-minded his second coup d'etat. This time there was no bloodshed, no popular protest. People were not in favor of the coup, but they hoped for more order in government and thought Batista could achieve it.

Batista had always believed that if people were well off

financially, they would be less inclined to bother with politics. Economically Cuba was in extremely good shape. Industry was flourishing, with new jobs being created every day. Still, most people were not satisfied with political conditions.

From the moment he took power, Batista made no pretense of his aims. He proclaimed himself a general and then claimed the presidency.

All of this led the intellectuals, politicians, and press to start a systematic campaign against the de facto government. Soon opposition was part of the life of a large sector of the people. Batista's first term of power, from 1934 to 1944, had been marked by greed. He and his friends had started as poor people and had finished as multimillionaires. Now the greed and government corruption were unprecedented. The repression in political matters was extremely harsh, and a feeling of despair was beginning to take hold in the people.

So how and why did the Communist revolution happen? In the first place, the takeover did not really begin as a Communist revolution. The Cuban people had suffered under years of corrupt government and were very eager for political change. They had the material means, the country was prosperous, and the driving force was the eagerness to find democracy again. There was no cohesion among the political groups, and Batista had suppressed freedom of the press by establishing periodical censorship of all newspapers, radio, and television stations. In fact, the opposition did not take hold until the attack now known as the 26th of July Movement. This attack was led by a young man named Fidel Castro. He and his men attacked the Moncada military fortress in the city of Santiago on July 26, 1953. It was a daring attempt to attract interest in their group, but it was a cruel action as they, in order to escape, went through the barracks hospital and killed a large number of personnel and injured many patients. The young men escaped to the nearby mountains where they were actively pursued by the army. After several days of fighting and many victims from both sides, the Roman Catholic archbishop of Santiago made the government promise that the rebels' lives would be spared if he brought them down from their hiding places in the mountains. The government kept its promise, and Fidel Castro, his brother Raúl, and a group of students and young professionals were tried and sentenced to three years in prison. Batista, to gain some popular support, commuted the sentence a few months later.

When he was released from prison, Castro went into exile in Mexico. It was there that he began recruiting young men with the purpose of overthrowing the Cuban government. In December of 1956, about eighty-five men of different ages and backgrounds landed in the eastern part of Cuba near the Sierra Maestra. There are many versions of what happened afterwards, and all that is known for certain is that many of the group perished in their attempt to go up the steep mountainsides. Only a small group of revolutionaries survived, among them Fidel and Raúl Castro and the Argentinian revolutionary Ernesto "Che" Guevara. From the Sierra Maestra the survivors began their guerrilla campaign against Batista's army. During the ensuing two years the guerrilla fighters grew in numbers, but they were always a small force. Meanwhile, the government forces were becoming more and more demoralized as might be expected of the military branch of a government that was rapidly crumbling in every other way.

While the army was battling Castro in the Sierra Maestra, Cuba's political parties were trying to reach a nonmilitary

Fidel Castro (left) training villagers in guerrilla warfare tactics and conferring with "Che" Guevara (right)

solution. The political parties wanted to form a coalition government that would include representatives from government, industry, labor, and other revolutionary factions under the leadership of Cosme de la Torriente. It would have been a good moment for Batista to leave with some dignity, but he refused to resign, and the revolution and guerrilla fighting went on.

The people, the middle-class in particular, were getting tired of the situation. They began to show their opposition to Batista in different ways. The economic and industrial sectors called for action against the regime. Batista always reacted with violence, and the situation was almost intolerable. Then the United States decided to withdraw its support from Batista. Seeing that he had no support either from within or outside his country, Batista fled Cuba with his close aides, family, and friends on New Year's Eve,

After taking control of Cuba in 1959, Castro (left) quickly turned it into a Communist state. Today Cubans honor Russian as well as Cuban revolutionaries in a May Day celebration (right).

1958. When the Fidelistas took control on New Year's Day, 1959, Cubans thought themselves a free people again.

The desire for honest, democratic government seemed to have crystallized, and at least ninety percent of the Cuban population joined in celebrating. Castro, a very clever man, had written a famous pamphlet titled "History will absolve me" before leaving Cuba for exile. This defense argument for his part in the Moncada attack was really a very shrewd political manifesto. The paper vowed to strive for national stability. At the same time it proposed advanced social reforms, but always within the framework of a democratic nation. For a short period this seemed to be true.

A WORSE TYRANNY: COMMUNISM

Castro made a few prominent men and women government officials. He promised a general election in the near future and was on friendly terms with the religious authorities. At the same time, he took measures that were highly socialistic and dictatorial. He always timed things so that on each occasion his action was the answer to some counter-revolutionary "attack." His intention was that the people would persuade themselves that whatever the government did was for the benefit of all.

Then Castro's government put into effect an agrarian reform that was quite different from the one that had been written with revolutionary lawyers while in the Sierra Maestra. This, and the fact that a great many soldiers and private citizens were shot by firing squads after being tried by the people's revolutionary tribunals made Cubans realize that they had wholeheartedly accepted a government that was a far cry from the democracy they had hoped for.

Castro, in the meantime, strengthened his personal power. His government took over hundreds of millions of dollars in United States property and privately owned businesses. It eliminated the rest of Batista's army, the labor unions, political parties, and professional associations. It abolished private schools and put all facets of education in the state's control. In every way, Castro's government took the place of the private sector in Cuban everyday life.

MANY CUBANS AWAKEN TO REALITY

It was at this point that the great exile began. Hundreds of thousands of Cubans who were dissatisfied with Castro's rule emigrated to Spain, the United States, and other countries, particularly those throughout the rest of Latin America. Spain and Latin America were obvious choices, because Spanish was spoken

Cubans requesting visas from the American embassy in 1960 (left) and seeking entrance to the United States in 1961 (right) through Florida.

and many Cubans had family ties in those countries. The United States, particularly the area in and around Miami, Florida, was another popular choice for several reasons:

1. Cuba is only ninety miles south of Florida, so it was the closest place to home the emigrés could find.
2. Traditionally, many Cubans had felt a great attraction for the United States. They had resented the "Platt Amendment," but had still enjoyed traveling to the States, and particularly to Florida and the metropolitan area of New York.
3. Cubans knew of the U.S. opposition to Communism and felt this country would be a congenial place to live while they waited for the moment to go back to a free Cuba.

The flight has never stopped. Out of a nation of less than eight million inhabitants, more than a million have left in the twenty-five years since Castro took command.

Castro's government has become totally allied with the Soviet

Union. The Soviet Union provides Cuba with all its petroleum requirements, all kinds of arms and ammunitions, machinery, and technical advice, and also food and medicine. It buys the major portion of Cuba's sugar crop, usually at prices above those of the free world market.

The Cuban government has become totally centralized. This means that all political parties were dissolved and replaced by the one-party system. The different revolutionary factions, the 26th of July Movement, the Revolutionary Directorate, and the Popular Socialist Party have been blended into one force, the Communist Party of Cuba. This party holds elections for local and provincial officials, who in turn elect the national leaders. The role of Castro has changed from army commander to prime minister and then to president.

Education has been a high priority of the Castro regime, and Cuba boasts the highest educational budget in Latin America. Education is free at every level, starting with pre-school and going all they way through middle or technical education. The educational system emphasizes workers' and technical education. There is even a system of health care for those who go on to the university level. The system's basic aim is the indoctrination of Communist ideals and goals.

Cultural life is also state-controlled. There is the National School of Fine Arts, attached to the art museum, the National Ballet School, the National Film Institute, and the Casa del Teatro, attached to the International Institute of Theater.

Health care is also free, but the new hospitals and clinics lack the specialized personnel and medicines needed for first-rate care. All doctors graduating from medical school must give time to the government by working in rural areas.

Caridad Theater in Santa Clara (above).
García Lorca Theater in Havana (above right).
Music room at the History Museum in Guanabacoa (below).
Museum of Art in Trinidad (below right)

Chapter 5

THE ARTS

Cuba's geographic position has always been an asset to the island. Ships going from North America to Central or South America usually stopped there which meant that Havana was privileged to receive many prominent artists. The performing arts have, therefore, always been important in this country. The major singers, instrumental soloists, and actors and actresses of the world have been seen and heard on the stages of Havana theaters. But Cubans are not just fortunate and appreciative audiences. They are also a nation of talented literary, musical, and visual artists themselves.

The Castro regime believes that mass culture is essential, and since 1959 the government has played a major role in structuring cultural life. A national council has been founded for fostering education in music, fine arts, ballet, dramatic arts, and modern dance. The government has also endeavored to bring cultural events to the provinces, where in pre-revolutionary Cuba cultural opportunities were limited, as well as to Havana. However, because of the difficulties and constraints put upon artists in a state-controlled society, a great many writers, poets, and other artists have left Cuba in search of liberty of expression. Of those

Novelist, Doña Gertrudis Gómez de Avellaneda (left)
and a statue of poet, José Martí (right)

who stayed behind, many have been or are still imprisoned in the dungeons of Cuba's ancient prisons, in the cells of the modern ones, or in concentration camps.

The history of the development of the arts in Cuba dates mainly from the last part of the eighteenth century and the beginning of the nineteenth. By that time Havana had become a capital city of major stature and when the winds of the Enlightenment that were blowing all over Europe reached Cuba's tropical shores, a variety of art forms began to flourish.

LITERATURE

THE NOVEL

First on the Cuban literary scene were the journalists who started publishing periodicals and newspapers by the 1790s. Most of the articles touched on sociological subjects and described the customs of Cubans at the time. Derivations of these articles became the first novels of the nineteenth century. Two women stood out as novelists of this era: Gertrudis Gómez de Avellaneda and the Countess of Merlin. The former wrote novels against slavery; the latter, description of her travels throughout the island. However, it is Cirilo Villaverde, whose novel *Cecilia Valdes* was the best seller of his time, who is considered the major novelist of that century.

In the twentieth century, several novelists and short story writers of international stature must be mentioned: Carpentier, Arenas, Cabrera Infante, and Labrador Ruiz. They, like many others, chose to leave their native land. Novas-Calvo is also recognized as a first-rate literary figure.

POETRY

Cubans seem to be born loving poetry; thus this land has given birth to many first-rate poets whose names shine in the roster of Latin American poetry.

During the nineteenth century a great number of Cubans wrote romantic poems, many of them while exiled. In general, these poems stressed the poet's homesickness for the far-off homeland, which was, in most cases, never to be seen again. Best known of all Cuban poets is José Martí, whose fame rests not only on his writings, but also on the fact that he is revered by all as the Father of Cuban Independence. Martí's beautiful lyrical poetry is memorized by every Cuban child, even the youngest. Heredia and Zenea are also prime examples of exiled poets who wrote from the countries to which they had been banished. However, early in the century, the poet known as "Plácido" had written a series of very patriotic poems in Cuba. Late in the nineteenth century, a form of poetry known as "modernism" took hold in Spanish-speaking

Cuban art reflects the vibrant colors of the surrounding landscape.

countries, under the influence of the French "Parnasian" poets. Julián del Casal stood out among the Cuban poets of this era. In twentieth century pre-Castro times, mention must be made of such poets as Emilio Ballagas, Mariano Brull, Eugenio Florit, Lezama Lima, and Nicolás Guillén.

The Castro Revolution, as was said before, brought out the poetic vein in many who opposed the regime and were sent to prison (from where they smuggled out their poems to be published in foreign countries) or managed to escape abroad. Among these are Valladares, Sales, Cuadra, Padilla, and Valls.

ART

Cuba is, like most tropical lands, a country of vivid colors and brilliant light. Many Cuban painters have made a name for themselves painting landscapes that reflect these varied colors and the lush exuberance of the tropics; in more recent times, many have acquired international renown by painting in an abstract manner.

Throughout Cuba paintings and sculptures adorn public places.

Although there were some attempts to paint in the early colonial period of Cuba, none of the artists were of sufficient stature to become well known. By the end of the nineteenth century, several good painters, such as Menocal, had appeared, but Cuban art really only became first-rate in the present century. Some of the better artists are known for their colorful renditions of typical Cuban scenes, artists like Víctor Manuel, Abela, and Amelia Peláez, to mention only a few. The abstract art movement is represented in Cuba, primarily, by Lam, an internationally acclaimed painter. Other great figures of modern art are Portocarrero, Bermúdez, and Mariano. Some very forceful sculptors have also made an impact on modern Cuban art; Sicre is one of them.

MUSIC

It is perhaps in the realm of music that Cubans have excelled over all other art forms. The Cuban people have two main lines of

Teacher directing a school band

heritage, Spanish and African. Spain as a country stands out musically. It has given the world not only great classical composers, but, perhaps even more importantly, an incomparable repertory of folk music. The Spanish musical tradition has remained strong in Cuba since Spanish colonial days. The other rich musical heritage in Cuba comes from the blacks. The number and variety of rhythms and melodies with an African origin is awesome. Thus in Cuba we find Spanish-type music, African-type music, and a mixture that derives from both, and has come to be known as Afro-Cuban music. Finally, there is the country folk music that is strictly Cuban.

We will speak only of some well-known composers, since the number of performers is so enormous. In the nineteenth century, light instrumental and voice pieces that had a characteristic beat and flavor were composed by men such as White, Cervantes, and Sánchez de Fuentes.

In the present century, Cuban music has flown beyond its borders, leaving the whole world singing and dancing to such Cuban melodies and syncopated rhythms as the rumba, the conga,

Traditional instruments are played on the street and in the home.

the bolero, the guaracha, the mambo, and the cha cha. Cuban songs have been translated into every language and have been incorporated into movies, plays, orchestra repertoires. Songs such as ''Siboney,'' ''Malagueña,'' ''Yours,'' to mention just a few, have gone around the world many times.

The instruments used to play Cuban music are not only the conventional ones found worldwide, but others that are entirely original and peculiar to Cuban musical groups. Some examples of these are the *güiro* which is made out of an oval-shaped dried fruit that must be rubbed with a stick. The *maracas* are also dried, round fruits that are filled with dried seeds or pebbles and shaken rhythmically. The *bongó* is one of many types of drums (actually twin drums bound together) on which goatskins are tightly

spread. They are played only by hand. *Claves* are two medium-sized sticks, each of which is held separately. Made out of a very hard wood called *acana*, they are beaten one against the other to mark a special beat. The bones of a donkey's jaw (*quijada de burro*) make an eerie noise that is also popular in Cuban musical groups.

One can also find in Cuba a number of folk songs and rhythms that cannot be classified as being of Spanish or African origin, but instead are strictly Cuban. These are the *guajira* (usually accompanied by guitar, claves, and maracas), the *criolla* (creole), the *son montuno*, and the *zapateo*. Most of these tunes are meant not only to be listened to, but to be danced to as well.

Among the great composers of the twentieth century one must mention Lecuona, Simón, Farrés, and Grenet.

*Cubans enjoy the rhythm of dance whether it is casual (left)
or part of a national dance company (right).*

Cuba is a country where music plays a very important part.
People play instruments, sing, and dance at the drop of a hat. At
the state level, the National Symphony Orchestra accompanies
opera and ballet and makes annual tours of the island.

DANCE

Dancing is ingrained in the soul of every Cuban. Nearly every
celebration, be it public or private, includes dancing. Small
children learn the intricate steps of Cuban popular and folk music,
and all Cubans take dancing seriously and are masters at
developing new steps and variations of a particular style. In the
rural areas, traditional folk dances are still popular. The most

famous one is the one called the *zapateo*. In the zapateo, the man wears white trousers, a pleated white shirt called a *Guayabera*, a triangular red kerchief around his neck, and a straw hat. The woman wears the *bata criolla*, a long, frilly dress (usually white with tiny red polka dots) that is shorter in front and has a sort of train in the back. This dress is a descendant of the *bata andaluza* worn by female Flamenco dancers in Spain.

Besides popular dancing, Cuba has always had a tradition of ballet. In the 1950s the Alicia Alonso Ballet School was created, as were some other smaller ballet schools. It was considered very much a part of a young girl's upbringing to take ballet lessons. Alicia Alonso, the Director of the School bearing her name, was an internationally renowned prima ballerina whose fame increased as years went on. Her husband, Fernando Alonso, was also a choreographer and ballet teacher of stature. Castro's government has continued the Cuban tradition of ballet dancing by giving full support to Alicia Alonso, whose school is now fully backed and subsidized by the state. Fernando Bujones is also a well-known Cuban ballet dancer who now lives in the United States.

FILM

Before the Revolution, film-making in Cuba could not be considered an art, as it was still in its primitive stages. After the Revolution, however, some young film-makers have made excellent films, most of which contain a veiled or overt message of Communist propaganda. The Institute of Cinematographic Art and Industry is very active, and several films made in Cuba have received international awards.

Ballet (left) and miming (right)

THEATER

The theater has always played an important role in Cuban life. In colonial days, one of the main cultural, as well as social forms of entertainment was attending one of Havana's many lovely theaters. Plays at the theaters were performed by foreign companies, mainly those from Spain, and sometimes from France. Local theater groups began springing up in the 1930s. Since the Revolution, Cuba has enjoyed a strong theatrical movement, with many plays organized by the Casa del Teatro under the sponsorship of the International Institute of Theater.

There has always been in Cuba a tradition for Spanish operettas called *zarzuelas*. In the nineteenth century several original Cuban zarzuelas were written.

The legendary Bodeguita del Medio restaurant (above) is near the
Cathedral Square in old Havana. Such famous people as Ernest Hemingway
have signed the walls to commemorate their visit. A variety of rice
and bean dishes usually accompany most Cuban meals (below).

Chapter 6

FOLKLORE AND CUSTOMS

FOOD

Cuba, like every other country around the world, has its own ways of preparing foods. Its cooking is based on the traditions inherited from Spain, on the influence of African cooking that came with the blacks, and on the fruits and vegetables that grow on the island.

Cuban food is highly seasoned but, unlike Mexican and other Latin-American cuisines, it is not hot, only spicy. Rice is a daily staple found on every Cuban family's table. It is often served plain (white) to accompany beans (usually black beans, although red and white beans are also popular). A variety of white rice and black beans cooked together is known as *moros y cristianos* (Moors and Christians), a reference to the Arabs who occupied Spain for many centuries. Another very delicious rice dish is *arroz con pollo* (rice with chicken), where yellow rice is mixed with tasty pieces of chicken, red pimento, and peas.

Picadillo is a dish made with ground beef, onions, green peppers, olives, raisins, and tomatoes. It is served with white rice, fried eggs, and fried ripe plantains.

Corn is also used in a variety of Cuban dishes. In many cases, it is not eaten on the cob, as it is in this country, but instead ground up and made into corn meal and cooked with pieces of pork. Cuban *tamales*, which taste quite different from their Mexican counterparts, are rolled into corn leaves and tied with a string.

Cuban hamburgers are called *fritas* and are much more highly seasoned before cooking than American ones, so they do not need mustard or catsup.

One of the very tasty Cuban soups is called *ajiaco*. It is a country dish made with a large variety of ingredients: vegetables such as *yucas, malanga, chayotes, ñames* (yams), and *boniatos* (sweet potatoes), with many different types of meat mixed in. We know that the original aborigines of Cuba also made ajiaco.

A highly seasoned sauce called *mojo* is made with minced garlic, olive oil, and sour orange juice and served with meats or sometimes vegetables. Mojo is served with *lechón*, a roast suckling pig, that is part of many festivities, especially Christmas Eve. In the country, the pig is often roasted outdoors on a spit.

It is impossible to talk about Cuban cooking without mentioning the high quality of seafood. From the tasty *Moro* crab to the *pargo* (red snapper), Cuba's waters are full of different varieties of fish and shellfish. Frogs' legs prepared in a garlic sauce are also popular.

Cuba being the largest sugar producer in the world, it is not strange that Cuban desserts are all extremely sweet. *Tocino del Cielo* (heavenly bacon), as well as *flan* come from Spanish cooking. Other desserts, like *Dulce de Leche* and *Buñuelos de Yuca*, are part of the Cuban traditional cooking.

A child's regular snack upon coming home from school is known as *Pan con timba*. This is a bread roll that has guava jelly

Tropical rum drinks (left) and Cuban coffee (right)

and cheese inside. Children often accompany this snack with a drink made with *gofio* (wheat germ).

Cuban rum is well-known the world over, and both dark and light rum are made there. The famous daiquiri cocktail made with light rum and green limes was popularized by Ernest Hemingway, the American novelist who lived in Cuba for many years and who won a Nobel prize in literature for his book about a Cuban fisherman, *The Old Man and the Sea*. Rum and Coca-Cola is also a well-liked drink known as a Cuba Libre.

Refrescos are Cuban nonalcoholic beverages (milkshake style) made with any number of the great variety of tropical fruits found on the island.

Coffee is one of the great Cuban gourmet delights. It is brewed differently than it is in the United States, closer to what is known here as expresso coffee and served in very small cups.

COCK FIGHTS

Cock fights are a typical Cuban form of entertainment. Just like horse races or dog races, it is a sport in which heavy betting is involved. The cocks used in these fights are trained to be fighters. They are bred separately from other cocks and their appearance is different since their feathers are shaved in a special way and their crests are cut. The cocks used for fighting belong to different breeds and, therefore, are of different color plumage.

The fights take place in a small arena called *valla*. The two fighting cocks are dropped in the valla, one in front of the other. The fight itself is similar to a boxing match. The owners and trainers stand by. The cocks go after their adversary with their spurs and the fight ends when one of the two cocks is either killed or "chickens out" by fleeing the valla. As many as ten or twelve cock fights take place in one afternoon. This sport that originated in the rural areas, later spread to the cities and has been a favorite pastime in Cuba since early days.

CELEBRATING RELIGIOUS FESTIVITIES

THE FEAST OF KINGS

Because of the many centuries during which Cuba was a Spanish colony, the Cuban population has kept many traditions from the mother country. One very important tradition was the celebration of the Feast of Kings or the Magi. This was the day of the year (January 6) when children received gifts that had supposedly been brought to them during the night by the Magi, the kings who came bearing gifts to the child Jesus. Parents would go shopping for toys on the night of the fifth, since all stores remained open until past midnight. The toys were put by shoes that the children had left out (just as stockings are hung in this country at Christmas time). Children who misbehaved got coal instead of toys.

Besides the Feast of Kings, Christmas was also celebrated as a family festivity, but the main meal, instead of being on December 25th, as it is in the United States, was served on Christmas Eve. This meal was usually followed by attendance at Midnight Mass, known as *Misa del Gallo* (Mass of the Rooster). Since the advent of the Communist regime in 1959, the Catholic religion has been curtailed. A great number of priests had to leave the country to avoid persecution, and attendance at church became a liability that could be punished by loss of job, harassment, and the like. This has changed somewhat in the last few years, with the government adopting a more lenient attitude toward the practice of religion. However, the Christmas celebrations and the Feast of Kings have been eliminated, and today presents are exchanged on July 26, which is the anniversary of the Revolution.

93

HOLY WEEK

Before the Revolution, Cubans kept very strictly the spirit of Holy Week, the week before Easter. It was a time of penance when one was not supposed to play music, go to parties, or attend movies.

In Havana and many smaller towns there were religious processions marching through the streets, in which someone dressed as Jesus Christ carried a cross and others carried statues of the Blessed Virgin on their shoulders. This, too, has disappeared since the Communist takeover.

CARNIVALS

Carnivals in Cuba have a very long tradition. They began as rowdy feasts in which people had fun and ate and drank abundantly before the beginning of Lent, during which they would fast for forty days. The tradition of celebrating Carnival (which is still kept in New Orleans, Rio de Janeiro, and other parts of the world) came to America from Europe. In Cuba it became a fantastic celebration in which the original Christian tradition was mixed with African music and rhythms.

People from each neighborhood would get together and plan a *comparsa* in which they would choose costumes and dances based on a specific theme. For example, the comparsa of the sultans would wear Arab costumes. Each comparsa had its own musical group and, on Carnival nights, they would parade down the streets dancing to strong rhythms, usually congas with a leader in the front carrying a long stick with a light on top called *Farola*. There would be a competition for the best comparsa, judged by an

Many parks line the parade routes that go through Havana.

official jury on the basis of costumes, music, and dance. There were also floats in the Carnival parade. The streets where the comparsas and floats passed were closed to traffic, and those who were lucky enough to live on those streets where the whole spectacle could be viewed would invite their friends and relatives to their house. It was a time of merrymaking and fireworks.

GOING AROUND AND AROUND

Until not too long ago, Cuban girls were not allowed to go out alone with boys. They had to be chaperoned by an older relative or a brother. For small-town girls, the way to see and be seen by the boys was to meet in the evening at the park (every Cuban town has a park that is the center of all activities). There the girls would link arms around each other's waists and walk around the park clockwise, while the boys made an outer circle and went around counterclockwise. If a boy happened to like a particular girl, he would wink or say something at the precise moment when he passed her as he walked around. Many a romance, and, later, marriage was started this way. This, as well as other old-fashioned customs, have almost disappeared in present-day Cuba.

Harvesting tobacco (above) and sugarcane (below)

Chapter 7

EARNING A LIVING

The new socialist system radically changed Cuba's economic philosophy and production methods. The normal western style of supply and demand economy, in which private enterprise is the main factor, was abolished, and a "planned" economy was put into effect instead. Based on Soviet five-year plans, the Cuban government, now owner of ninety-eight percent of the land and of all means of production, set long-range goals for the manufacture of goods. These goals frequently go unmet, and even though some progress has been made, rationing of most products, even sugar, is still a national way of life.

Cuban economy has been based since early days on four basic products: sugar, tobacco, coffee, and cacoa. Of these four, sugar was brought in by Spanish colonists from the Balearic Islands, but tobacco, coffee, and cacao were endemic to the island.

Sugarcane thrived in the rich Cuban soil, and the colonists understood that this was one of the most valuable assets of their new land. Cuba was called the "sugar bowl of the world" and of the approximate seven million tons of sugar produced in an average year, about sixty-two percent was sold to the United States, the United Kingdom, and other European nations. The rest was distributed for local consumption and to other parts of the world. The Soviet Union has become Cuba's most important buyer during the last twenty-five years.

The production of sugar is an involved process that begins with the planting of sugarcane. Harvesting requires a large number of skilled cutters, and having only unskilled cutters has been one of the problems faced by the present government in its drive for higher tonnage production. Cane must be cut at a certain height from the ground and in a certain way to ensure proper growth in the next season. A sugarcane plant may grow back for up to fifteen years, but higher yields are realized by rotating the fields and planting a new crop every five to seven years. Watching the cutting of sugarcane by a group of skilled workers is like watching a ballet. Their movements are rhythmic and graceful. They hold the cane with one hand while they raise the machete (a wide, one-edged steel tool) with the other to cut the cane with one stroke and then trim the leaves off with another stroke. They then cut the stalk into pieces and throw them on a pile that reaches just a certain height, before the cutter goes on to start a new pile. Modern machinery has helped sugarcane harvesting and made it more efficient, and sugarcane cutting as a skilled occupation is becoming obsolete. After harvesting, sugarcane pieces are transported to the mill and crushed to produce the juice that is called *guarapo*. Guarapo goes through a process of evaporation and is then boiled at very high temperatures until it becomes a syrup called *melado* (molasses). This thick brown liquid is then passed through enormous centrifuges and precipitated into raw sugar. Raw sugar is dark brown, thick and moist. Some sugar mills

A sugar plantation (right) and sugar refinery (left)

continue processing the sugar until it is refined—that is, until it has become small, pure white crystals. There are many mills that do not continue with this process. Sugar from these mills is then transported to other mills called refineries. The sugar used in making industrial candy is usually not totally refined.

There are many by-products of the processing of sugar. For example, bagasse, the fiber left after the extraction of the guarapo, has several different uses. The most important use is as a fuel in the same industry. A second is in paper processing. Most Cuban newspapers have used bagasse paper for many years.

Another very important by-product of sugar processing is distilled liquor. There is a high-quality liquor, rum, that is an important industry in Cuba, Puerto Rico, Jamaica, Aruba, and the Virgin Islands. Other lower-graded liquors are also distilled on these islands, but these are not usually exported. Alcohol (not the beverage kind) made from molasses is another by-product.

Tobacco has traditionally been the second most important agricultural product of Cuba. Though tobacco is native to most of

The art of hand-rolling cigars is quickly giving way to machine-made products

the subtropical and tropical regions of the North American continent, Cuban tobacco is considered to be of a very special quality and has been a major source of wealth in the agricultural and industrial economy of the country.

To produce high quality tobacco leaves a very select plant must be harvested. Many laborers are required to care for the plants, which must be cut at a precise time and then tied together in small groups that are then hung to dry in the *casa de tabaco* until they reach a degree of dryness that makes the rolling possible. A hand-rolled cigar is considered a real delicacy among smokers and has always been sold at a much higher price than the machine-made kind.

Cigars are hand-rolled by *torcedores*. These are traditionally men who work at tables where they pick the tobacco leaves one by one and roll them to make the highly sought-after cigars. From very early times up to the present these workers have been entertained while working by readers called the *lectores de tabaqueria*. These men had to be good readers, but they also had to have very strong voices in order to be heard by all four hundred to five hundred people working in the large factory room. Traditionally the readers chose from novels like *The Tale of Two Cities* by Dickens or the *Count of Monte Cristo* by Dumas, or many other works by Spanish writers. At present they read only modern Russian novels or from speeches by Castro.

The manufacture of most cigars and cigarettes has been a mechanized process for many years. The process is automated from the moment the leaves are picked up from the casa de tabaco to the moment the cigars and cigarettes are packed and ready to be shipped to the places where the product is sold. But hand-rolled cigars are still made by the process that requires a person doing a job with care and pride.

Coffee and cacoa, are grown on mountainous terrain, and although Cuba is over sixty percent lowland, the high yield and fertility of its hillsides made both products important. The process of growing coffee in commercial plantations was started by a group of French and British settlers. Coffee is still grown in Cuba, but the cultivation of cacoa has been almost entirely abandoned in the last decades.

Aside from these traditional agricultural products, modern Cuba produces a number of crops that have been important during the last forty years. Among these are rice, corn, plantains, bananas, and a large variety of vegetables that are used both for local consumption and as exports.

The cattle industry is of great importance in Cuba. High-grade

Fruit pickers (left) after a long day of work. A nice catch of fish (right)

beef was always available from Cuban cattle, and concerted efforts resulted in high-quality milk products as well. Virtually all milk, butter, and cheese consumed on the island are produced by Cuban dairy cows.

FISHING AND OTHER INDUSTRIES

Cuban waters are home to a very large variety of fish and shellfish, but until recently the fishing industry had not been organized. The socialist government has created an official fishing fleet and fisheries with large hatching and spawning areas. As a result, fish has become a major source of food and an important item in the national economy.

Something similar may be said of the poultry industry, and even though chicken is still difficult to find in a normal family's table, its production has changed and poultry raising has become an organized industry.

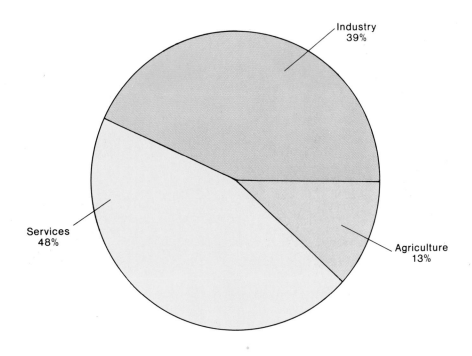

Industry
39%

Agriculture
13%

Services
48%

Leather processing as an industry has grown tremendously after its very modest start during late colonial times. Though many things are made from leather—purses, wallets, belts, briefcases, suitcases, and saddles—the shoe manufacturing industry is the most important. The high-fashion kind were often imported, but the shoes worn regularly by the majority of the population are made in Cuba. Shoes are also exported in large enough quantities to make this industry very important.

TEXTILES

Processing of textiles has been for many years a major industry in Cuba. It has traditionally employed a large sector of the working force. There are several large textile factories, with the Rayonera de Matanzas (the largest and most successful) producing nearly half of all textiles used in Cuba.

A day care center in Batabanó, one of Cuba's southern cities.

SOCIAL SERVICES

Social service industries fall in three main categories: day-care institutions for pre-school children, women's organizations, and nursing homes.

Salaries and prices in social services are set by the state and controlled very rigidly. Workers do not have real freedom to choose where they work, as they are usually assigned to a certain working facility by the government.

TOURISM

Tourism was once Cuba's third major industry, but it slackened considerably after the 1959 revolution. Today Castro's government is trying to rebuild the tourism industry, and to a certain extent it has succeeded. There are tours available from European countries, but the American tourist trade is still nonexistent. In its attempt to revitalize the industry, the government has built some new facilities in Varadero, Isla de la Juventud, and other places.

Chapter 8

SPORTS

There is one field in which Cuba has changed drastically since 1959, and that is in sports. As in all socialist countries, there are no professional sports in Cuba, and sports events are completely government controlled.

The favorite sport in Cuba is baseball. It has been the most popular one ever since the early days of the republic. If there is an empty lot anywhere and two kids nearby, you will soon see them pitching and batting with a baseball bat, or a stick, or even just their hands—but they will be playing some form of baseball! Before the revolution of 1959 their aim was probably to become good enough players to make it into the professional leagues. There were several Cuban teams that had close links to the minor and major leagues in the United States.

Many U.S. teams—the Cincinnati Reds, the Washington Senators, the Chicago White Sox, and the Boston Red Sox to name just a few—had scouts in Cuba and signed many young prospects into the minor leagues to try them out before assigning them to major league teams. Adolfo (Dolf) Luque was one such prospect. Luque was a pitcher for the Cincinnati Reds for eleven years. In 1923 he had 27 wins and struck out 127 batters. Orestes (Minny)

Baseball greats such as Cuba's José Canseco (left) once competed on grade school teams as these (right).

Miñoso of the Chicago White Sox was another outstanding Cuban player. He played both center field and third base and was a powerful slugger during the 1950s and early 1960s. Two other Cuban players of the same period include pitcher Camilo Pascual, who won 174 games for the Washington Senators, and Tony Oliva, a leading outfielder and slugger for the Minnesota Vikings.

During the 1986 U.S. baseball season José Canseco, who played outfield for the Oaklands A's, led his league in homeruns and runs batted in. Canseco was born in Havana in 1964 and now lives in the United States. There have been many other fine Cuban baseball players, though not all achieved the same level of fame. Besides the professional teams founded at the beginning of the twentieth century, there were hundreds of amateur teams, sponsored by clubs, schools, businesses, and the like. Wherever there were Cubans, there were baseball teams!

Boxing is also quite a popular sport in Cuba, attracting young men from all groups of society. But while middle- and upper-class young men might have boxed primarily for the sport of it, men from lower-class families saw amateur contests as stepping stones to becoming professionals.

Minnie Miñoso   *Adolfo Luque*   *Chocolate Kid*   *Gavilán Kid*

Boxing has been described as the most difficult sport of all, since it requires a perfect physical condition, unusual muscle strength, and exceptional agility, as well as a quick mind to help the boxer determine what to do during every second of the contest. But boxing is also one of the most dangerous sports, where bodily injuries are not a result of accidents, but derive from the very nature of the sport. That is why although many try boxing, only a few actually become well-known figures.

In Cuba boxing is practiced extensively, and many amateur boxers have gained international recognition, both before and after the 1959 revolution. Some of Cuba's better-known boxers include Chocolate Kid, Gavilán Kid, Benny Parets, and Teófilo Stevenson, who became the Olympic heavyweight champion.

Court games like tennis, squash, racketball, and handball have always been played in Cuba, but only by a small minority of the population. One court game that is universally popular is basketball (*baloncesto*). All Cuban high schools and colleges have basketball teams, and many others are sponsored by various clubs.

Other than baseball, field sports have never enjoyed much popularity in Cuba. Rugby football was played for a very short season during the winter months, but it could never compete with baseball. And soccer was and is still a game without an audience. Before 1959 it was played mainly among the teams of the Spanish regional clubs. There are more soccer teams today, but it is still not a popular game.

Volleyball used to be an intramural sport, but has been restructured into a nationally organized women's and men's sport.

Track and field is a very popular sport. It has given Cuba many winning figures, including the 1977 Olympic Champions of the 100- and 110-meter race. The 800-meter winner that year was also Cuban. Alberto Juantorena was an immensely popular figure because he had taken part in other championships, always winning the highest honors. More recently, Silvia Costa was the 1985 Olympic champion in high jump, and Ivonne Leal won the javelin-throwing world medal.

Among water sports swimming, diving, and rowing have always been popular competition sports, but they have become much better organized in the last few years. Other team sports like water polo have never been popular.

Cycling is a brand-new organized sport in Cuba. Several different competitive cycling races throughout the year culminate in the Cycling Around the Island competition—La Vuelta a Cuba—an international event in which many Communist countries participate yearly.

Chess and dominoes are also very popular. Cubans have always enjoyed playing chess. José Raúl Capablanca was the international

Workers relax over a game of chess during their lunch break.

chess champion from 1921 to 1927. In recent years chess has been greatly promoted through the required cultural exchanges with the U.S.S.R., and by means of the Soviet technical advisers who are so common on the island.

Dominoes is second only to baseball in popularity—and some Cubans say it is even more popular. Baseball is an organized team game, while dominoes can be played informally by just two to four people. It can be enjoyed by all age groups, playing at all times of the year. Cuban dominoes, a perfect example of the influence of Spanish culture, do not stop at double sixes, but go on until double nines. Having so many more pieces makes the game more complex and challenging, and it is loved by almost everyone.

A very popular court game of the spectator kind is jai alai. Jai alai is one of the fastest court games. It is played by tossing a very hard ball back and forth, using a basket that is strapped to the player's hand. The players work so hard that they lose an average of five pounds per game. Jai alai originated in the Basque region in Spain, and the best players, called *pelotari*, still come from there.

A wonderful variety of people and customs make up Cuba.

EPILOGUE

This lovely country with all its traditions, its natural beauty, and its wonderful people was once only a short flight away for the many Americans who visited it frequently or who made it their home. It is now a remote place that we hear about only occasionally from people with conflicting opinions. Perhaps at some time in the near future we will be able to see all the things we have talked about and will be better able to understand Cuba and its people.

OUTSTANDING CUBANS

1. GERTRUDIS GÓMEZ DE AVELLANEDA (1814-1872)
Born in Camagüey Avellaneda is considered one of the foremost Romantic writers in the Spanish language. Her first poems were published in 1841 under the title *Poesías Líricas*. These poems reveal some of the suffering she endured in her lifetime and show, at the same time, her romantic vision. Some of her novels have an anti-slavery theme, while her plays are, for the most part, based on historical themes.

2. "PLÁCIDO" (Gabriel de la Concepción Valdés) (1809-1844)
A romantic poet born in 1809, he died a martyr's death, executed by the Spanish government in Havana after the "Escalera" conspiracy in 1844. "Plácido" (his pen name) was a mulatto born of a black father and a Spanish mother and raised in an orphanage. He learned the combmaker's trade working as an apprentice. Despite his deficient formal education, his were some of the best poems written by a Cuban in the nineteenth century. Many of these poems were cries for Cuba's independence.

3. FATHER FÉLIX VARELA (1788-1853)
A great thinker of the nineteenth century whose life was a model to a whole generation of Cubans, Varela was born in Havana in 1783. He became a priest and dedicated his life to trying to form a national conscience in his countrymen and to instill in them sound ideas of independence. His revolutionary ideas, coupled with the fact that he had an enormous following, led the Spanish administration in Cuba to consider him a political threat. He was, therefore, banished to the United States. While living in the States he continued to perform his priestly duties and, at the same time, published a magazine called "The Habanero," which was circulated clandestinely in Cuba and which Spanish officials called *opúsculos incendiarios* (explosive pamphlets). He died in the United States in 1853. That same year, José Martí, the man who was to carry the torch of freedom, was born in Havana. The Cuban philosopher, José de la Luz y Caballero, said of Varela: "He was the first person who taught Cubans how to think."

4. JOSÉ DE LA LUZ Y CABALLERO (1800-1862)
One of Cuba's foremost educators, Caballero was born in 1800. He was educated in Havana both at its university and at its seminary. From an early age, he was recognized as a learned scholar. He became a professor of philosophy at the seminary but later decided to teach at the elementary level. Eventually, he would be instrumental in the founding of the Normal School of Havana, where teachers learned their profession. As a journalist, he did not hide his revolutionary ideas and hopes for a free Cuba. José de la Luz y Caballero led an exemplary life and stands out as a beacon of light in the intellectual community of the nineteenth century.

5. JOSÉ ANTONIO SACO (1797-1879)
José Antonio Saco was born in Cuba in 1797 and is considered one of the greatest influences in the formation of the Cuban national character. He became a distinguished writer, sociologist, historian, and precursor of the revolutionary thought that was to flourish during the next century.

He published extensively in scientific and political fields. His *Historia de la Esclavitud* (History of Slavery), is still used by historians. Cubans see Saco as the prototype of an honest, brilliant man who gave his countrymen his best effort in bringing them a philosophy of dedication to the betterment of human enterprise.

6. JOSÉ MARÍA HEREDIA (1803-1839)
This great Cuban poet was born in Santiago de Cuba in 1803. As a young lawyer, he worked for the independence of Cuba. Having been warned of his imminent arrest, Heredia left his fatherland secretly, never to return. He lived in the United States for a while, and there wrote his famous "Ode to Niagara." Then he settled in Mexico and worked as a judge, a teacher, and a journalist. He died when he was only 36. Heredia's verse reflects a constant nostalgia for his country, as well as a strong exhortation for Cubans to join the ranks of freedom fighters. His most famous poem, "Hymn to the Exile," became the rallying cry of Cuban patriots who had to live abroad. Heredia is considered one of the major lyricists and romantic poets of Latin America.

7. IGNACIO AGRAMONTE (1841-1873)
One of the most romantic figures, as well as a famous military genius of the Ten Years' War, Agramonte was a young, handsome lawyer from Camagüey. He early on joined the ranks of the rebels and quickly made his position known: he wanted an abrupt break with the past, a total abolition of slavery, a separation of state and church, and the establishment of a federal republic. When Agramonte fully comprehended that his radical ideas were not accepted by the majority of Cubans led by Céspedes, he became a military leader. General Agramonte was killed in action in 1873. His death was an enormous loss to the cause of Cuban independence.

8. ANTONIO MACEO (1845-1896)
Known as "The Bronze Titan" because of his strength, courage, and fierce spirit, Maceo was born of mixed blood in Santiago de Cuba. His mother, a patriotic woman, instilled in him the virtues that would make him a great leader. He and his brother began to fight for independence in 1866. By 1876, Antonio was the military leader of the eastern part of Cuba. He never accepted the peace treaty signed at Zanjón in 1878 and thus became a perennial fighter. Maceo was killed by a bullet in 1896, after receiving twenty-six wounds. One of his most famous sayings was: "One does not ask for freedom. One conquers it with the blade of the machete."

9. JOSÉ MARTÍ (1853-1885)

Born in Havana of a modest family, young Martí was sentenced at age sixteen by the Spanish government to six years of hard labor in a marble quarry for being the editor of a revolutionary paper and for supporting Cuban independence. After serving part of his term, he was exiled to Spain, where he studied law. From there, he went to Mexico and Guatemala and began his writing career, returning to Cuba after the Peace of Zanjón. Shortly thereafter, he was again exiled because of his revolutionary activities. This time he went to New York, where he labored incessantly for the cause of Cuban independence, uniting for the first time the military leaders who had fought during the Ten Years' War. He founded the Cuban Revolutionary Party, which was joined by many exiled Cubans, and he raised money for the cause. A man of great integrity and personal charisma, Martí was truly the inspiration and leader of all Cubans who longed for freedom. After he was killed on the battlefield, he became even more of a symbol and a martyr to the cause.

10. MÁXIMO GÓMEZ (1836-1905)

Máximo Gómez was born in the Dominican Republic in 1836. As a youngster, he joined a group of rebels in a battle against Spain, but the attempt failed. He then migrated to Cuba and after a short while joined the revolutionary forces that were engaged in the Ten Years' War. He was among those that did not accept the terms that ended the war.

When the revolutionary forces began their last attempt to free Cuba from Spain, he returned as head of the military forces. He was a great strategist and successfully commanded the ill-equipped Cuban forces against the fully-armed Spanish army. Even though he was highly respected by the Cuban people, he refused to participate in any political contest. He believed he had served his adopted nation the best way he could and went into retirement for the rest of his life. He died in Havana in 1905, just four short years after the establishment of the republic.

11. CARLOS J. FINLAY (1833-1915)

Yellow fever, an epidemic disease of the tropics, used to be one of the worse dangers faced by people in tropical lands. In the wars of independence it was responsible for more soldiers' lives than were bullets. This dreaded disease is no longer a problem, thanks to the discoveries of a Cuban physician, Dr. Carlos J. Finlay. Throughout his career, Dr. Finlay had studied yellow fever patients and researched its transmission. Finally he reached the conclusion that it was caused by the bite of mosquito.

Finlay presented his discovery at an International Sanitary Conference. The U.S. Army Commission undertook the eradication of mosquitoes in Cuba and Panama and was so successful that it can be said it ended the yellow fever danger all over the world.

Dr. Carlos J. Finlay was born in Cuba in 1833, graduated from Jefferson Medical College in Philadelphia in 1855, and in 1879 was appointed by the Cuban government to work on yellow fever research. He became chief sanitation officer in Cuba in 1902. Finlay died in Havana in 1915.

12. COSME DE LA TORRIENTE (1872-1954)

Torriente, born in 1872, was a statesman and a diplomat. He fought in the War of Independence and, later, as Cuban Ambassador to the United States, he was instrumental in bringing about the release of the Isle of Pines to Cuba by the American government. Torriente became President of the League of Nations headquartered in Geneva, Switzerland, and, in 1950, was named Honorary President of the World Federation of the United Nations Associations. Near the end of Batista's dictatorship Torriente headed the commission which tried to find a peaceful solution. He was universally applauded for his honesty and integrity.

13. GAVILÁN KID (1926-   )

Gerardo González, Gavilán Kid, was born in 1926 in the city of Camagüey, but his family moved to Havana when he was quite young. In 1943 he made his boxing debut in that city. He was extremely fast and soon became famous for his ''bolo'' punch. Gavilán became welterweight champion in 1952. Gavilán defended his title four times before losing to Johnny Saxton. During his twelve years in the ring, Gavilan was never knocked out.

14. KID CHOCOLATE

Eligio Sardiñas, Kid Chocolate, the first important figure in Cuban boxing, was born in Havana. He started boxing very early, and by 1922 had challenged the world junior lightweight title. He became world champion in 1931 and was declared world featherweight champion in 1932.

Kid Chocolate had a style all his own, which he used to great advantage in the many matches he fought during his peak years. He retired from the ring in 1936, when the Cuban government gave him a pension and a job as official boxing promoter. The Kid is a national hero, the first Cuban boxer of international stature and a national inspiration to many young men of less affluent means.

15. JOSÉ RAÚL CAPABLANCA (1898-1942)

Capablanca was born in Havana in 1898. He was a good baseball and tennis player, but his real loves were the more intellectual games of bridge and chess.

Capablanca graduated from Columbia University in New York City and later joined the Cuban diplomatic service, a move that enabled him to travel widely. He mastered his chess playing and in 1921 became world champion. He retained the title until 1927.

Capablanca's style was deceptively simple. Even after losing the title, he played for many years making his defeat of other masters look easy. He died in New York City in 1942.

MAP KEY

Alto Cedro	D6	Ens. de la Broa (bay)	C2,3	Nueva Gerona	D2
Antilla	D6	Florida	D4	Nuevitas	D5
Arch. de los Colorados		Fomento	C4	Old Bahama Channel	
(archipelago)	C1,2	Gibara	D5	(channel)	C,D4,5
Archipiélago de Sabana-Camagüey		Golfo de Ana María (gulf)	D4	Oriente (province)	D,E5,6
(archipelago)	C3,4	Golfo de Batabanó (gulf)	C2	Palma Soriano	D5,6
Artemisa	C2	Golfo de Guacanayabo (gulf)	D5	Palmira	C3
Atlantic Ocean	B5,6	Golfo de Guanahacabibes (gulf)	C,D1	Penin. de Zapata (peninsula)	C3
(inset map)	D,E2,3	Guanabacoa	C2	Pico Turquino (mountain peak)	D5
Banes	D6	Guanajay	C2	Pinar del Río	C2
Baracoa	D6	Guane	C1	Pinar del Río (province)	C2
Batabanó	C2	Guantánamo	D6	Placetas	C4
Bayamo	D5	Guayabal	D5	Pta. de Prácticos (point)	D5
C. Corrientes (cape)	D1	Güines	C2	Puerto Padre	D5
C. Francés (cape)	D2	Güira de Melena	C2	Quemado de Güines	C3
C. San Antonio (cape)	D1	Gulf of Mexico (gulf)	B,C1,2	Regla	C2
Cabo Cruz (cape)	E5	Havana	C2	Remedios	C4
Cabo Lucrecia (cape)	D6	Holguín	D5	Sagua de Tánamo	D6
Cabo Maisi (cape)	D6	I. de Pinos (island)	D2	Sagua la Grande	C3
Caibarién	C4	Jagüey Grande	C3	San Antonio de los Baños	C2
Caimanera	D,E6	Jardines de la Reina (islands)	D4	San Juan y Martínez	C2
Camagüey	D5	Jatibonico	D4	San Luis	D6
Camagüey (province)	D4,5	Jovellanos	C3	Sancti-Spíritus	D4
Camajuaní	C4	Júcaro	D4	Santa Clara	C4
Campechuela	D5	La Esperanza	C2	Santa Cruz del Sur	D4,5
Candelaria	C2	La Habana (province)	C2,3	Santa Fé	D2
Caonao (river)	C,D4	La Rioja	D5	Santa Lucía	D6
Cárdenas	C3	Largo (island)	D3	Santaren Channel (channel)	B,C4
Caribbean Sea	D4	Las Villas (province)	C,D3,4	Santiago de Cuba	D6
(inset map)	E1,2,3	Los Palacios	C2	Sierra Maestra (mountains)	D,E5
Casilda	D4	Manzanillo	D5	Straits of Florida (straits)	B,C3,4
Cauto (river)	D5	Marianao	C2	Tiguabos	D6
Cayo (island)	D3	Martí	D5	Trinidad	D4
Cayo Romano (island)	C4,5	Matanzas	C3	Tunas de Zaza	D4
Ciego de Avila	D4	Matanzas (province)	C3	U.S. Naval Base	D6
Cienfuegos	C3	Mayarí	D6	Unión de Reyes	C3
Colón	C3	Minas	D5	Victoria de las Tunas	D5
Consolación del Sur	C2	Morón	C4	Windward Passage	D,E6,7
Corralillo	C3	Nicholas Channel (channel)	C3,4	Yaguajay	C4
Cruces	C3	Niquero	D5	Zaza (river)	C,D4
Ens. de Corrientes (bay)	D1				

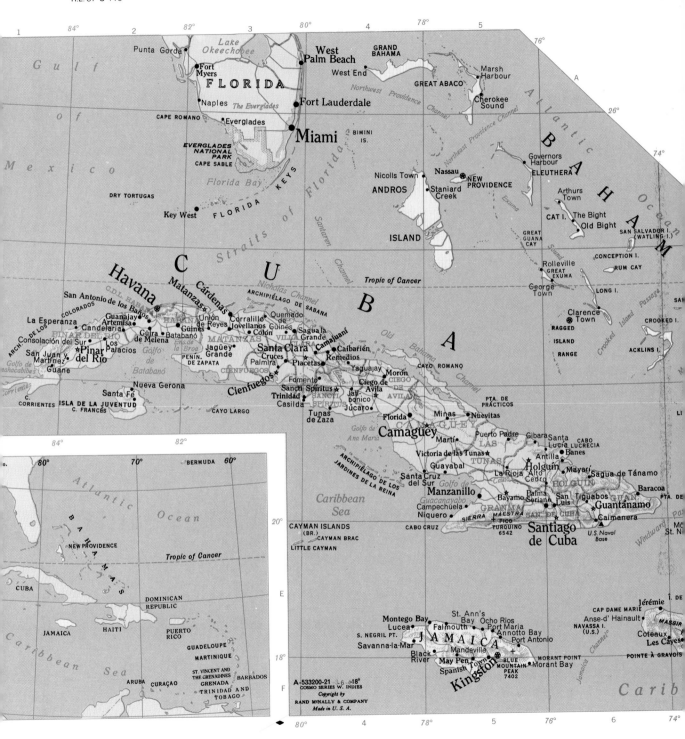

Statute Miles 25 0 25 75 125

Kilometers 25 0 25 75 125 175

Oblique Conic Conformal Projection
SCALE 1:6,000,000 1 Inch = 95 Statute Miles

MINI-FACTS AT A GLANCE

GENERAL INFORMATION

Official Name: República de Cuba (Republic of Cuba)

Capital: Havana

Official Language: Spanish

Government: The constitution adopted in 1976 established Cuba as a socialist state and a republic. In fact, however, Cuba is a dictatorship controlled by Fidel Castro and the Communist party.

The National Assembly is the supreme legislative organ; it usually meets twice a year. It delegates its functions to a council of state which is the real center of power. The president of the council serves as both head of state and head of government.

Cuba has a system of popularly elected provincial assemblies. Cubans 16 years and older have the right to vote.

National Anthem: "La Bayamesa"

Flag: Officially adopted in 1902; it consists of blue and white stripes, with a red triangle on the left with a white star in the center.

Money: The basic unit is the peso. One peso equals 100 centavos. The peso is not a freely exchanged currency against the U.S. dollar.

Weights and Measurements: Cuba is officially on the metric system.

Population: Estimated 1989 population—10,540,000

Major Cities:

	1981 Census	1988 Estimate
Havana	1,924,886	2,059,223
Santiago de Cuba	345,772	389,654
Camagüey	245,238	274,974
Guantánamo	167,405	192,590

Religion: Cuba is a Catholic country, though few people attend church with any regularity. The socialist government has forced many priests to leave the country. Black religious practices have mixed with elements of Catholic worship into a religion called *ñañiguismo,* which resembles the Voodoo religion of Haiti.

GEOGRAPHY

Highest Point: Turquino Peak, 6,476 ft. (1,974 m)

Lowest: Sea level

Coastline: 2,100 mi. (3,380 km)

Mountains: The western mountains, the Cordillera de Guaniguanico, has two ranges, the Rosario and the Sierra de los Órganos, whose parallel ranges resemble the pipes of an organ.

The Sierra de Trinidad in the southern central part of the island includes the Trinidad range and the Sierra del Escambray. Extreme eastern Cuba is extremely mountainous and is divided into northern and southern ranges by the Guantánamo Valley.

Rivers: There are many rivers, but most of them flow a short course and carry little water. The one exception is the Cauto which has many tributaries. The rivers are on the whole not used for navigation, but there are many scenic streams and waterfalls.

Climate: Temperatures range from 72 degrees F (22 degrees C) in January to 82 degrees F (28 degrees C) in August. There is a rainy season from May to mid-November and a dry season from November through March. Mid-June to November is the hurricane season.

Greatest Distances: Northwest to southeast, 759 mi. (1,221 km); north to south 135 mi. (217 km).

Area: 42,804 sq. mi. (110,861 km²)

NATURE

Trees: The royal palm is the national tree of Cuba. Its bark is used to build the typical rural house. Dried-out leaves are used for roofing.

The ceiba (kapok) has cottonlike flowers that are used to fill pillows and mattresses. Its bark is used for medicinal purposes.

Pines grow in many parts of the island.

Other trees include coconut, mango, avocado, guava, and papaya, as well as orange, lemon, and grapefruit.

Hardwoods are being slowly reforested, and mahogany, ebony, and granadillo are yielding increasing amounts of valuable timber.

Fish: More than 500 edible species exist in Cuban waters, including red snapper, grouper, sea bass, swordfish, and tuna, and there are 37 varieties of shark alone. There are far fewer freshwater fish.

Animals: Reptiles are distributed equally among sea, river, and dry-land species. Marine species include the tortoise and the hawkbill turtle; mud turtles and crocodiles inhabit marshes. Frogs and toads are prevalent. Thirty species of bats prey on mosquitos and insects harmful to agriculture.

Birds: More than 300 species and subspecies of birds can be found in Cuba, though deforestation has damaged the bird habitat greatly. Parrots are abundant, as the birds of prey. Typically Cuban species include the flamingo, royal thrush, nightingale, mockingbird, and hummingbird.

EVERYDAY LIFE

Food: Cuban food is based on Spanish traditions, but it is also influenced by African elements brought by the blacks and by the native fruits and vegetables that grow on the island.

Rice is found daily on the Cuban table; sometimes it is mixed with tasty pieces of chicken, pimento, and peas (*arroz con pollo*).

Picadillo is made with ground beef, onions, green peppers, olives, raisins, and tomatoes.

Corn is also used in many Cuban dishes—not on the cob, but ground and made into cornmeal and cooked with pieces of pork.

Seafood is prevalent and is high in quality.

Rum and coffee are among the most popular drinks.

Housing: the larger cities have an acute housing shortage and improved housing is one of the priorities of the Castro regime. Two or more families may share an apartment. A large number of country people live in thatched huts with cement floors.

Holidays and Celebrations:

January 1—Anniversary of the Revolution
January 28—Birthday of José Martí
Four weekends before Ash Wednesday—Carnival
May 20—Republic of Cuba Day
July 24-26—Founding of Santiago de Cuba
July 26—Beginning of the Castro revolution
December 7—Commemoration of all national martyrs
December 24—Christmas Eve
December 25—Christmas Day

Culture: The culture of Cuba is Hispanic, with strong African overtones in folklore, music, and dance. Cuban literature was greatly influenced by the century-long struggle for independence. José Martí, the national hero and apostle for freedom, was a prolific author and wrote on every aspect of North American life. He was perhaps the best interpreter of the United States that Latin America had. E.J. Varona was the island's foremost philosopher and Julian del Casal its best modernist poet.

The love affair between the Spanish guitar and the African drum gave Cuba its characteristic musical forms—the rumba and the song. Hispano-Cuban music, however, consisted of many ballads and romantic songs. Havana has an excellent Philharmonic orchestra.

A flourishing film industry has developed under the auspices of the Cuban Institute of Cinema Art and Industry founded by the government in 1959.

Ballet is flourishing, although live theater has tended to lag. The National School of Fine Arts has produced excellent painters, who are highly individualistic, though influenced by the French. Picasso's African period has been a particular source of inspiration to contemporary artists. The greatest sculptor is Juan José Sicre, a professor at the National School of Fine Arts.

After 1959 Castro devoted considerable amounts of support to book publishing and efforts to bring culture to the masses. A series of international writers' congresses won the support of many Latin intellectuals for the Cuban revolution.

Sports and Recreation: Cubans are avid sports fans and especially enjoy baseball, basketball, swimming, and track and field. Jai alai and cockfighting are also popular. The Castro government has greatly encouraged sports development, and Cuban participation in the Olympics and other international competitions has improved markedly since 1959.

Communication: Radio stations, television stations, and the country's 10 daily newspapers are controlled by the government. Major Cuban cities are connected by telegraph and telephone lines, but many homes do not have telephones.

Transportation: Total road mileage increased by 50 percent during the 1960s. Automobile transport has been downgraded with increasing emphasis on truck and bus transport.

In 1959 there was a small merchant fleet of 14 ships, but sixteen years later cargo capacity had increased about 19-fold. There was a corresponding increase in foreign commerce.

The railroad system deteriorated in the years after the revolution, but was being restored by the mid-1970s.

The state airline, Cubana, flies within Cuba and operates some international flights.

Schools: The eradication of illiteracy was given high priority by the revolutionary government. Dissolution of private schools was one of the new government's first acts and a state-directed educational system was set up. Education is free at all levels. It includes 12 grades preceded by a preschool; higher, or university education; adult and technical education; and specialized education.

Health: Medical care is free, and mortality rates are gradually being reduced. The official ratio of doctors to the population was 1:1,000 in 1974, considered an acceptable rate in underdeveloped countries. Physicians are required to work in rural areas for two years after completing their training.

Social Welfare:: Homes for the aged are under the direction of an organization called Minsap (Ministry of Public Health), but day care is organized under the Federation of Cuban Women which also supervises more than 8,000 social workers.

ECONOMY AND INDUSTRY

Chief Products: Agriculture—cattle, citrus fruits, bananas, pineapples, coffee, sugar cane, tobacco, vegetables. Manufacturing—cement, cigarettes, cigars, fertilizers, rum, textiles. Mining—limestone, chromite, iron, nickel, manganese, cobalt, copper.

IMPORTANT DATES

1492—Columbus lands in Cuba and claims the island for Spain

1517—The first slaves arrive in Cuba

1868-78—Cuban revolutionaries fight in the Ten Years War. Spain promises reforms

1886—Slavery abolished in Cuba

1895—A revolution breaks out, led by José Martí

1898—Spanish-American War—Spain gives up all claim to Cuba

1898-1902—U.S. military government controls Cuba

1902—Estrada Palma becomes the first president of Cuba

1906-09—American forces occupy Cuba for the second time, after open rebellion against Estrada Palma government

1933—Batista takes control; his hold lasts until 1959, except for the years 1944-52.

1959—Castro leads unsuccessful attack on Moncada Army Barracks in Santiago de Cuba.

1961—Exiles invade at Bay of Pigs but are repulsed by Castro's forces

1962—Russia accedes to U.S. insistence that it withdraw its missiles and missile bases

1971—United States announces that Russia agrees not to establish permanent submarine base in Cuba

1976—Cuba adopts new constitution; Cuba declared socialist state and a republic

1977—United States ends travel restrictions to Cuba

1980—About 125,000 Cubans arrive in the United States

1982—United States reinstates travel restrictions to Cuba

1986—Start of immigration pact, which allows the United States to give entry to 27,000 Cubans a year and to deport some Cubans who entered the United States illegally in 1980

1987—Cuban teams participate in the Pan American games held in Indianapolis, Indiana

1989—Cubans celebrate the 30th anniversary of the revolution that brought President Fidel Castro to power.

IMPORTANT PEOPLE

Agramonte, Ignacio (1841-73), one of the most romantic figures of the Ten Years War

Alonso, Alicia, founder of National Ballet Academy

Avellaneda, Gertrudis Gómez de (1814-73), famous poet, playwright, and novelist

Barnet, Dr. José A., became president of Cuba in 1935

Batista, Fulgencio, took hold of Cuban government in 1939 and established dictatorship

Capablanca, José Raoul (1888-1942), world champion chess player

Casal, Julián del (1863-93), Cuba's foremost modernist poet

Casas, Friar Bartolomé de las, (1474-1566), Dominican monk who came to Cuba with Velazquez

Casas, Luis de las, Cuba governor who was a model of justice and honesty; rated best governor Cuba ever had

Castro, Fidel, came to power in 1959, established socialist state in Cuba

Céspedes, Carlos Manuelé de, declared independence of Cuba in 1868

Cortés, Hernán, helped Velazquez conquer Cuba

Countess of Merlin, wrote descriptions of travels around the island in the nineteenth century

Estrada Palma, Tomás first president of the Republic of Cuba, 1902

Finlay, Carlos Juan (1833-1915), Cuban doctor who demonstrated that yellow fever was transmitted by the mosquito

García, General Calixto, organized uprising called the "small war" in 1879-80

Gómez, José Miguel, second president of Cuba (1909-13)

González, Gerardo [Gavilan Kid] (1926-   ), welterweight champion

Guillén, Nicolás (1902-   ), poet of strong African rhythms whose work reflects a strong interest in social justice

Heredia, José María (1803-39), great revolutionary poet, one of the country's best lyricists

Hernandez Catá, A. (1885-1941), writer of psychological short stories

Lopez, General Narciso, made several attempts in the 1850s to start revolution of liberation

Loveira, Carlos (1882-1928), realistic novelist

Luz, José de la (1800-1862), one of Cuba's foremost educators, founder of the Normal School of Havana

Machado, General Gerardo, took office in 1925; one of the most tyrannical leaders in Cuban history. He died in March, 1939.

Martí, José, national hero and apostle of the struggle for independence

Martínez Compos, General Arsenio, Spanish governor who arrived in 1871 and instituted a number of reforms

Menocal, Mario García, president of Cuba, 1913-21

Ocampo, Sebastián de, followed coasts of Cuba by ship in 1509 and discovered it was an island

Plácido [Gabriel] de la Concepción Valdés (1809-44), Romantic, lyrical poet

Saco, José Antonio, Cuban thinker who wrote against slavery

Sardiñas, Eligio [Kid Chocolate], first important figure in Cuban boxing

Sicre, Juan José, greatest Cuban sculptor

Soto, Hernando de, sixteenth-century governor of Cuba who left island in 1539 to conquer Florida

Torriente, Cosme de la (1872-1954), statesman and diplomat, became president of the League of Nations

Varela, Father Félix (1788-1853), role model to a whole generation of Cubans; revolutionary thinker

Varona, E.J. (1849-1933), Cuba's foremost philosopher

Velázquez, Diego, led conquest of Cuba for Spain

Villaverde, Cirilo, author of *Cecilia Valdés*, major novelist of the nineteenth century in Cuba

Zayas, Alfredo, president of Cuba (1921-25)

INDEX

Page numbers that appear in boldface type indicate illustrations

About the Authors

Rosa E. Casas was born in Havana, Cuba. She received her bachelor's degree in language education from the University of Havana and her advanced degree from the Catholic University of Villanueva in Cuba. Mrs. Casas taught junior high school in Cuba for fifteen years.

Since leaving Cuba in 1961, Mrs. Casas has worked at *Encyclopaedia Britannica*. The mother of five children, Mrs. Casas lives with her family in the Chicago area.

Ana Maria Brull Vasquez was born in Cuba. Because her father was a Cuban diplomat, she lived with her family in many other countries. A graduate of the University of Ottawa in Canada, Mrs. Vasquez received her master's degree in history from the University of Fribourg in Switzerland. Upon her return to Cuba, she directed the manuscript department of the Lobo Napoleonic Museum in Havana, developed radio programs for the Ministry of Education, and wrote numerous magazine articles for Havana magazines. Forced into exile because of the Communist takeover, Mrs. Vasquez worked as associate editor of *The Guidepost*, an American magazine published in Madrid, Spain.

A resident of Chicago for twenty-five years, Mrs. Vasquez has been a freelance writer for radio and television, an editor and translator, a college Spanish teacher, and a volunteer worker for a variety of cultural programs. She has raised her three children, Alejandro, Isabel, and Jaime, in a totally bilingual and bicultural environment.

Mrs. Vasquez was recently awarded the Cross of Queen Isabella of Spain by King Juan Carlos I in recognition of her accomplishments.